The Ultimate Good Energy Cookbook

365 Days of Wholesome Recipes Inspired by Dr. Casey Means to Rev Up Your Metabolism, Burn Fat, and Boost Your Health | 28-Day Meal Plan Included

Kate Hines

Table of Contents

CHAPTER 6 48

Wind Down with Wholesome Dinners 48

CHAPTER 7 61

Energy-Boosting Snacks 61

INTRODUCTION

When I set out to write the *"Good Energy Cookbook,"* I was driven by a very personal goal: *finding ways to unlock better, more sustainable energy in my own life.* Like so many people, I found myself constantly fighting sluggishness and fatigue, even after getting what I thought was enough sleep. It became clear that the food we eat plays an incredibly significant role in how energetic we feel throughout the day.

My journey into understanding the link between food and energy began a few years ago. I'd wake up feeling groggy, struggle through work with multiple cups of coffee, and crash on the couch by the evening. It wasn't until I started paying closer attention to my diet that I saw a notable difference. What we put into our bodies isn't just about calories or weight management; it's about fueling ourselves for whatever comes our way.

It became evident that certain foods provide a steadier supply of energy than others. For example, complex carbohydrates break down slower, providing more sustained energy compared to simple sugars which offer quick but brief boosts followed by crashes. Lean proteins and healthy fats also play a vital role in keeping our energy levels stable.

But it wasn't just about discovering what foods to eat; it was equally important to understand how these foods interact with each other within a balanced meal plan. This is why throughout the book; you'll see recipes designed with balance and variety in mind. From metabolism-boosting breakfasts to protein-packed lunches and wholesome dinners, each recipe is carefully crafted to help you maintain good energy levels.

Another inspiration came from looking at lifestyle factors contributing to low energy levels — stress, lack of physical activity, poor sleep hygiene — and how food can help mitigate these issues. For instance, while developing recipes like the *Almond Butter and Banana Toast* or the *Quinoa and Avocado Power Bowl*, I considered ingredients known for their benefits in promoting good sleep or reducing anxiety.

I also wanted this cookbook to be practical for everyday living. It's easy to recommend exotic superfoods or complicated dishes, but what really makes a difference are recipes that fit seamlessly into your lifestyle without demanding too much time or effort. That's why I included practical tips on stocking your pantry and selecting high-energy snacks, so you're always prepared no matter how busy life gets.

Finally, sharing these discoveries felt important because maintaining good energy isn't just about being awake; it's about being present for your loved ones, handling daily responsibilities efficiently, and having enough left over at the end of the day for yourself.

So here it is: a collection of delicious recipes all aimed at helping you achieve stable energy levels. The "*Good Energy Cookbook*" is more than just food; it's about bringing vitality back into your life one meal at a time.

Enjoy your read,

Kate Hines

CHAPTER 1
The Science of Good Energy

Metabolism And Its Role in Energy Levels

When we talk about metabolism, we're referring to all the chemical processes that occur within our bodies to maintain life. Every action your body performs, from moving your muscles to thinking and even breathing, relies on metabolic processes.

Now, metabolism is divided into two main categories: *catabolism* and *anabolism*. **Catabolism** is the process where our body breaks down food and nutrients to produce energy. On the other hand, **anabolism** involves using this energy to construct and repair cells. You can think of catabolism as breaking down a Lego structure into individual blocks (to release energy) and anabolism as using those blocks to build something new (to grow or repair cells).

Metabolism provides the energy needed for everything we do. Whether we're resting or working out, it's our metabolism that ensures our body has the necessary energy to function properly.

How Does Metabolism Affect Energy Levels?

Your body's main goal is to maintain a stable internal environment, often referred to as homeostasis. Metabolism plays a critical role in this by ensuring you have enough energy to perform daily activities—everything from breathing and thinking to exercise and digestion.

When your metabolism is running smoothly, your body can efficiently convert food into energy, which keeps you feeling active and alert. However, when there's a glitch in this system—say due to hormonal imbalances or nutritional deficiencies—you may feel sluggish or fatigued.

Your **Basal Metabolic Rate (BMR)** is also worth mentioning here. BMR refers to the number of calories your body needs just to perform basic functions at rest, like keeping your heart beating and lungs breathing. The higher your BMR, the more calories you burn at rest, resulting in better energy levels throughout the day.

Several factors can influence your metabolism:

1. Age: As we age, our metabolism tends to slow down. This means our bodies become less efficient at converting food into energy.
2. Muscle Mass: Muscle tissue burns more calories than fat tissue even while at rest. This means that individuals with more muscle mass generally have higher metabolic rates.
3. **Physical Activity:** Regular exercise can boost your metabolic rate by building muscle mass and increasing oxygen consumption post-exercise.
4. **Genetics:** Genetics play a role too; some people naturally have faster metabolisms.
5. **Hormonal Balance:** Hormones like thyroid hormones play a vital role in regulating metabolic rate.

If you eat more calories than you burn through physical activity or at rest (BMR), those extra calories get stored as fat, leading to weight gain and potentially lower energy levels because excess weight can make physical activity more strenuous.

On the flip side, if you're not eating enough or skipping meals frequently, your body might think it's in *"starvation mode"* and slow down your metabolism to conserve energy. This can leave you feeling tired and less energetic because your body isn't efficiently converting food into the fuel you need.

By paying attention to these factors, you can help support and possibly enhance your metabolism, keeping yourself energized throughout the day. And remember, small changes can add up over time, making a big difference in how you feel and function every day.

Common Myths Debunked About Metabolism

There are so many myths and misconceptions floating around about metabolism that it's hard to sift through what's true and what's not. So, let's break down some of these myths together!

Myth #1: Skinny People Have Faster Metabolisms

One of the most common myths is that thin people have faster metabolisms, while those who are heavier have slower ones. But the reality is quite different. Metabolism is influenced by several factors, including your age, sex, muscle mass, and even genetics. Skinny doesn't automatically mean a fast metabolism just like being heavier doesn't mean you're doomed to a slow one. It's more complicated than that.

Myth #2: Eating Small Meals Frequently Boosts Your Metabolism

You've probably heard that eating six small meals a day can keep your metabolism revved up. The truth is, the frequency of your meals doesn't have a significant impact on your metabolic rate. What matters more is the total amount of food you consume and its nutritional quality. So, whether you eat three big meals or six small ones, your metabolism will burn the same number of calories.

Myth #3: Exercise Alone Can Speed Up Your Metabolism

Don't get me wrong—exercise is fantastic for a plethora of reasons, but relying on it solely to speed up your metabolism isn't a good strategy. While regular exercise can increase your muscle mass and subsequently boost your resting metabolic rate (RMR), it's essential to pair it with proper nutrition and adequate rest for optimal results.

Myth #4: Metabolism Doesn't Change with Age

People often think once you're past a certain age, you're stuck with whatever metabolism you have for life. But that's not true! While it is common for metabolic rates to slow down as we age due to decreases in muscle mass and changes in hormonal levels, this decline can be slowed with a healthy lifestyle. Regular strength training, proper nutrition, and staying active can help maintain muscle mass and keep your metabolism more vibrant as you age.

Myth #5: You Can't Change Your Metabolism

Many folks believe they are simply born with a specific metabolic rate and there's nothing they can do to change it. The good news is that's not entirely true! Lifestyle choices play a huge role in determining our metabolic health—exercise routines, dietary habits, sleep patterns—all contribute significantly. While you can't change everything about your metabolism (thanks to genetics), you certainly have control over improving aspects of it.

Myth #6: All Calories Are Created Equal

Okay, this one always gets people talking. Yes, from a purely energy standpoint, a calorie is just a unit of energy. But when we look at how different foods affect our bodies in terms of hunger management, nutrient absorption, and overall metabolic health—the type of calories you consume matters greatly! 100 calories of almonds are not the same as 100 calories from soda in how they influence your body processes.

Myth #7: Fasting Will Ruin Your Metabolism

Many people fear that skipping meals or intermittent fasting will put their bodies into *"starvation mode,"* causing their metabolism to plummet. While it's true that prolonged severe calorie restriction can lower your metabolic rate over time as part of a survival mechanism—it takes quite extreme conditions for normal intermittent fasting protocols to do that. In fact, intermittent fasting done correctly has shown promising benefits in maintaining lean muscle mass and supporting fat loss without drastically affecting metabolic rate.

Benefits of a Good Energy Diet

If you're like me, you're always looking for ways to feel your best, both physically and mentally. Eating the right foods can really make a world of difference. Below are the top benefits of sticking to a good energy diet.

Improved Physical Health

When you fuel your body with the right nutrients, it's like giving your car premium gas instead of regular. You can expect better performance, fewer breakdowns, and a longer-lasting engine. Eating a diet rich in whole foods like fruits, vegetables, lean proteins, and whole grains helps your body function at its best.

These foods provide essential vitamins and minerals that strengthen your immune system, making you less susceptible to illnesses. Plus, they're packed with antioxidants that help fight off harmful free radicals – those sneaky little particles that can cause damage to our cells and accelerate aging.

Enhanced Mental Clarity and Focus

Have you ever felt foggy or struggled to concentrate? Your diet could be playing a big part in that. Certain foods can help enhance brain function. For instance, omega-3 fatty acids found in fish like salmon are great for brain health. They support cognitive function and memory.

Leafy green vegetables like spinach and kale are loaded with vitamins E and K, which have been linked to slower rates of cognitive decline as we age. Nuts and seeds provide healthy fats that are essential for brain function. Here's another quick reference for mind-boosting foods:

FOOD	WHY IT'S BENEFICIAL
Fatty Fish	High in omega-3 fatty acids
Leafy Greens	Rich in vitamins E & K
Berries	Contain antioxidants
Nuts & Seeds	Provide healthy fats
Whole Grains	Steady release of glucose keeps energy levels stable

Weight Management and Overall Well-being

A good energy diet doesn't mean starving yourself or following extreme diet plans. It's all about making balanced choices that nourish your body while keeping you feeling satisfied. Foods high in fiber – like whole grains and legumes – help you feel full longer because they take more time to digest. This means fewer cravings for snacks. Lean proteins do the same because they're more satiating compared to carbs or fats.

Also, staying hydrated is important. Sometimes we think we're hungry when we're actually just thirsty. Drinking enough water also helps regulate metabolism and aids in the digestion process. Don't underestimate the power of regular meals with consistent eating times; it helps keep your blood sugar levels stable which can prevent overeating.

CHAPTER 2
The Good Energy Principles

The Good Energy Cookbook is about more than just cooking; it's a way of living that emphasizes nourishment, balance, and joy. We focus on making food that's not only delicious but also brings good vibes and energy to our lives. Here are some core principles:

1. **Balance**: It's not just about food; it's about maintaining harmony in everything we do. When it comes to meals, balance means incorporating a variety of nutrients - carbohydrates, proteins, fats, vitamins, and minerals. Think of your plate as a colorful palette where every section plays a role in your overall health.

NUTRIENT	EXAMPLE FOODS
Carbohydrates	Brown rice, quinoa, sweet potatoes
Proteins	Chicken breast, tofu, lentils
Fats	Avocado, olive oil, nuts
Vitamins	Leafy greens, berries, citrus fruits
Minerals	Nuts, seeds, legumes

2. **Seasonality**: Eating seasonal foods ensures that you're getting the freshest produce available while also being kind to the environment. Seasonal fruits and veggies are packed with more nutrients and taste better because they've ripened naturally. Plus, it's fun to look forward to what's in season!

3. **Simplicity**: Good food doesn't have to be complicated. Simple recipes with fresh ingredients can be incredibly satisfying and nourishing. Using fewer but higher-quality ingredients often results in better-tasting dishes.

4. **Mindfulness**: Eating mindfully means paying attention to what you're eating and how it makes you feel. This includes listening to your body's hunger signals and eating when you're genuinely hungry rather than out of habit or boredom.

> ➤ Take time to chew and savor each
> ➤ Focus on your meal without screens or work

> ➤ Think about where your food came from
> ➤ Eat when hungry, stop when satisfied

5. **Whole Foods**: Emphasize whole foods over processed ones. Whole foods are those that are as close to their natural form as possible – think fruits, vegetables, whole grains, nuts, seeds – basically anything that grows from the ground or comes from a tree!

Whole foods tend to contain more nutrients than their processed counterparts and are free from added sugars, unhealthy fats, and artificial ingredients.

6. **Hydration**: Good hydration is essential for maintaining energy levels. Make sure to drink plenty of water throughout the day. Herbal teas and other low-sugar beverages can also help keep you hydrated.

ACTIVITY LEVEL	DAILY WATER INTAKE (APPROX)
Sedentary	8 cups (64 oz)
Moderately Active	9-11 cups (72-88 oz)
Very Active	12-15 cups (96-120 oz)

7. **Community**: Food has a unique way of bringing people together. Share meals with family and friends whenever possible. This not only makes the meal more enjoyable but also builds stronger relationships and enhances your overall well-being. Sharing food is a form of expressing love and care, and it also provides an opportunity to learn from others' food habits and traditions.

8. **Moderation**: Everything in moderation is a good mantra to live by, especially when it comes to food. Indulging in your favorite treats is perfectly fine as long as it doesn't become a regular habit. The key is to enjoy those moments without guilt while maintaining a healthy overall diet.

FOOD TYPE	EXAMPLE TREATS	MODERATION TIPS
Sweets	Chocolate, cookies, ice cream	Enjoy once or twice a week
Salty Snacks	Chips, pretzels	Opt for smaller portions
Rich Dishes	Creamy pastas, fried foods	Balance with lighter meals

9. **Variety**: Variety isn't just the spice of life; it's essential for a nutritious diet. Eating a wide range of foods ensures you get all the nutrients your body needs. Try new recipes, incorporate

different vegetables, fruits, grains, and protein sources to keep your meals interesting and well-rounded.

Following these core principles can help you create meals that boost your energy levels and make you feel great from the inside out. Remember, the *Good Energy Cookbook* isn't just about cooking – it's about enjoying life through the food we eat and the company we keep.

How Nutrition Impacts Metabolic Health

I've always believed in the saying, *"You are what you eat."* But have you ever wondered why that's true? Everything we eat gets transformed inside our bodies into something useful. *Ever think of your body as a factory?* It's constantly working to convert food into energy. Just like a car needs fuel to run, our bodies need the right kind of food to stay energized.

When we talk about *"good energy,"* we're not just talking about those days when everything seems to click into place and you feel like you can take on the world. We're also talking about the literal energy that powers every single cell in your body, allowing you to move, think, and even breathe.

The primary form of energy that our cells use is called ATP (*adenosine triphosphate*). Think of ATP as the gasoline that powers your body's engine. Just like a car won't run without gas, your cells can't perform their vital functions without ATP. So, *where does ATP come from?* Every bite of food we eat provides the raw materials our bodies need to produce ATP. However, not all foods are created equal when it comes to fueling this energy process efficiently.

Have you ever noticed how some meals leave you feeling sluggish while others make you feel upbeat and ready to tackle anything? That has a lot to do with how different nutrients affect your metabolic health—the intricate process by which your body converts food into energy.

1. **Carbohydrates:** These are your body's main source of energy. They're like high-octane fuel for your car's engine. Simple carbs like sugar give you quick energy, while complex carbs like whole grains offer long-lasting power.
2. **Proteins:** Proteins repair and build tissues, which is essential for maintaining good energy levels. Imagine them as the construction workers fixing up your body's "wear and tear."
3. **Fats:** It might surprise you, but fats are not the villains they are often made out to be. Healthy fats, like those found in avocados and nuts, provide slow-burning energy that can keep you going all day.
4. **Vitamins and Minerals:** These guys might be small but don't underestimate their power! They help in over a hundred roles within your body, including converting food into energy.

a) *Iron:* Iron helps carry oxygen throughout your body. Without it, you'd feel sluggish and tired.

b) *Magnesium:* This helps with hundreds of biochemical reactions in the body, including breaking down glucose into energy.

c) *B Vitamins:* The B gang – B6, B12, riboflavin – helps to unlock the energy from foods.

d) *Vitamin C:* This vitamin does more than boost your immune system; it also improves iron absorption.

NUTRIENT	FUNCTION	GOOD SOURCES
Carbohydrates	Main source of rapid or sustained energy	Whole grains, fruits
Proteins	Repairs/builds tissues	Lean meats, beans
Fats	Provides slow-burning energy	Avocados, nuts
Iron	Carries oxygen for better energy	Spinach, red meat
Magnesium	Supports biochemical reactions	Dark chocolate, leafy greens
B Vitamins	Unlocks energy from foods	Eggs, dairy
Vitamin C	Boosts iron absorption	Citrus fruits

Other Lifestyle Factors That Contribute to Energy Levels

We all know that eating right and staying active can boost our energy, but have you ever felt that something was still off even when you were doing everything *"right"*? That's because there are many other lifestyle factors at play in our overall energy ecosystem. Understanding these additional elements can give you a more rounded approach to manage your energy levels better.

Life isn't just about eating kale salads and running marathons. It's also about managing your emotional well-being, surrounding yourself with positive influences, and creating a space that promotes mental peace. When you pay attention to these aspects, you're less likely to experience those inexplicable slumps in energy.

If you're only focusing on diet and exercise, you're ignoring the role stress, relationships, and even your living environment play in your energy levels. Sustainable energy comes from a holistic approach that combines multiple lifestyle factors. Time is precious, and understanding all these factors can help you streamline your approach to maintaining high energy levels.

1. **Stress Management**: Stress is unavoidable, but how we manage it can make all the difference. When I'm feeling overwhelmed, I've found that taking a few deep breaths or practicing mindfulness can help center me. Engaging in hobbies that I enjoy or just stepping back to slow down can significantly reduce my stress level. Effective stress management helps mitigate fatigue and keeps both my mind and body energized.

2. **Social Connections**: Having a strong support system is essential for maintaining high energy levels. Spending time with friends and family can be incredibly rejuvenating. Whenever I feel drained, connecting with my loved ones often recharges me emotionally and physically. These social interactions provide a sense of belonging and emotional stability, which in turn boosts my overall energy.

3. **Nature Exposure**: Being outdoors has an almost magical effect on my energy levels. Whether it's a hike in the woods or just a stroll in the park, nature has a calming presence that refreshes me instantly. The fresh air and natural light work wonders for alleviating stress and improving mood, which directly impacts how energetic I feel.

4. **Digital Detox**: In this age of constant connectivity, our devices can be both helpful and draining. I've noticed that taking regular breaks from screens – whether it's turning off my phone for an hour or avoiding social media in the evenings – helps me reset mentally. This digital detox allows my mind to clear up any fogginess and makes me more present and energetic during my day.

5. **Sleep**: We all know how vital sleep is, yet it's often the first thing we sacrifice when life gets busy. Consistently getting 7-9 hours of quality sleep has transformed how I feel each day. Creating an evening routine – maybe reading a book or taking a warm bath before bed – signals to my body that it's time to wind down, ensuring better rest and higher energy levels the next day.

6. **Hydration**: It's amazing how something as simple as drinking enough water can influence our energy levels so profoundly. Whenever I start feeling sluggish, it often turns out I haven't had enough water for the day. By keeping a bottle handy and aiming for at least 8 glasses daily, I stay hydrated which significantly boosts my focus and stamina.

7. **Personal Space**: Having a dedicated space where I can retreat to recharge is essential for maintaining my energy levels. Whether it's a corner of your home filled with your favorite things or just organizing your environment to reduce clutter – these personal spaces serve as sanctuaries where you can quietly reflect and reboot whenever needed.

By paying attention to these lifestyle factors, I've been able to keep my energy levels consistent throughout the day. Incorporating these simple yet effective habits into your daily routine may help you experience the same benefit too!

The Glycemic Index and Its Importance In Maintaining Energy Levels

So, what exactly is the glycemic index? Picture this: every time you eat, the food you consume has a specific impact on your blood sugar levels. Some foods cause a spike in blood sugar, while others release sugar slowly and steadily into your bloodstream. The glycemic index (GI) is a scale from 0 to 100 that tells you how quickly those sugars from the food get into your bloodstream. Think of it as a speedometer for food—you know, like those speed limits for driving!

GI VALUE	CLASSIFICATION
0-55	Low GI
56-69	Medium GI
70-100	High GI

When we eat high-GI foods, like white bread or sugary snacks, our blood sugar spikes rapidly. This might give us a quick burst of energy, but it's followed by a sharp crash. We've all felt it before: that mid-morning slump or post-lunch drowsiness where our energy just plummets. It's no fun at all! On the other hand, low-GI foods release glucose more slowly and steadily, providing a more constant source of energy throughout the day. Foods like whole oats, lentils, and sweet potatoes fall into this category. Eating them helps us avoid those nasty crashes and keeps our energy levels more balanced.

Why Does Glycemic Index Matter?

1. **Stable Energy Levels:** When we aim for low-GI foods, we get a steady supply of glucose to our brain and muscles. This helps us stay more alert and active without those sudden drops in energy.
2. **Better Focus:** Ever tried concentrating after eating too much candy? Not easy, right? Low-GI foods can help maintain concentration and mental performance since they avoid drastic fluctuations in your blood sugar.
3. **Feeling Full Longer:** Low-GI foods usually take longer to digest, which means they keep you feeling full for longer periods.

FOOD ITEM	GI VALUE	CATEGORY
White Bread	75	High GI
Brown Rice	55	Low GI
Apple	40	Low GI
Corn Flakes	81	High GI
Chickpeas	28	Low GI

So, imagine starting your day with something high in energy but low on the GI scale—a bowl of steel-cut oatmeal topped with fresh berries can be an excellent choice. You'd be setting yourself up for stable energy through the morning rather than crashing before lunch.

But hey, life's too short to think that you'd never touch a piece of white bread again! The great thing about understanding the glycemic index is that it gives us choices. We can mix high-GI foods with low-GI options to create balance in our meals.

CHAPTER 3
Building a Good Energy Pantry

Stocking Your Kitchen

Stocking your kitchen with the right ingredients can make a world of difference in how you feel every day. Think of your kitchen as the control center for your health and vitality. Fill your pantry with everything you need to keep your energy levels high and steady.

1. **Whole Grains:** Whole grains like brown rice, quinoa, oats, and whole wheat pasta are great staples. They're rich in complex carbs which provide a slow but steady release of energy throughout the day.

    a) *Brown Rice:* A versatile side for many dishes.

    b) *Quinoa:* High in protein and cooks quickly.

    c) *Oats:* Perfect for breakfast, keeps you full till lunch.

    d) *Whole Wheat Pasta:* A healthier alternative to white pasta.

2. **Proteins:** Proteins are essential for repairing tissues and maintaining muscle mass which is also key in keeping up our energy levels.

    a) *Eggs:* Packed with proteins, vitamins D & B12.

    b) *Chicken Breast:* Lean protein source that's easy to cook.

    c) *Tofu/Tempeh:* Great plant-based proteins rich in iron and calcium.

    d) *Legumes (lentils, chickpeas):* Full of fiber and protein, perfect for soups or salads.

3. **Healthy Fats:** Don't fear fats! Healthy fats like those found in avocados, nuts, and olive oil provide sustained energy and are essential for brain health.

    a) *Avocados:* Great on toast or in salads.

    b) *Nuts & Seeds (almonds, chia seeds):* Perfect snacks; add to yogurt or salads.

    c) *Olive Oil:* Use it as a dressing or for cooking; it's high in healthy monounsaturated fats.

4. **Fruits & Vegetables:** These should be the bulk of your diet as they provide essential vitamins and minerals. Aim for a colorful variety – each color often signifies different nutrients!

    a) *Leafy Greens (Spinach, Kale):* High in iron and calcium.

    b) *Berries (Blueberries, Strawberries):* Excellent sources of antioxidants.

c) *Citrus Fruits (Oranges, Grapefruits):* High in vitamin C; boosts immunity.

d) *Sweet Potatoes:* Rich in fiber and Vitamin A; superb roasted or mashed.

5. **Hydration Essentials:** Sometimes fatigue is just dehydration. Keep yourself hydrated to maintain your energy levels throughout the day.

a) *Water:* The most basic yet most important fluid.

b) *Herbal Teas (Peppermint, Chamomile):* Good alternatives if you want something warm without caffeine.

c) *Coconut Water:* Natural electrolytes make it great post-exercise.

Boosting Your Day with Superfoods for Energy

Superfoods are basically nutrient-rich foods considered to be especially beneficial for health and well-being. They are packed with vitamins, minerals, antioxidants, and other essential nutrients. Here's some of the energy-boosting superfoods you should know about:

1. **Chia Seeds**: These tiny black seeds are a powerhouse of nutrition. They're rich in omega-3 fatty acids, proteins, and fiber. Toss them in your smoothie or yogurt; they're energy boosters that keep you full longer because of their high fiber content. Plus, they stabilize blood sugar levels which helps maintain your energy throughout the day.

2. **Quinoa**: Quinoa is a complete protein that contains all nine essential amino acids. It's also loaded with iron and magnesium, both of which are crucial for energy production. Try it as a base for your salads or as an oatmeal alternative in the morning.

3. **Spinach**: We've known from cartoons that spinach makes you strong like Popeye—and there's some truth to that! Spinach is high in iron, which is important for transporting oxygen in your blood. More oxygen means more available fuel for your muscles and brain.

4. **Sweet Potatoes**: With their natural sweetness and creamy texture when cooked, sweet potatoes are easy on the digestive system and provide sustained energy because they have complex carbohydrates. They're also high in vitamin C and manganese.

5. **Blueberries**: These berries might be small but they're jam-packed with antioxidants and vitamins such as vitamin C and K. They help reduce oxidative stress in our bodies, which can otherwise sap our energy levels.

6. **Green Tea**: While tea might not be a "*food*," it's worth mentioning here because it can give you a natural energy boost without the jitters associated with coffee. Green tea contains L-theanine, which works together with caffeine to improve cognitive function and focus.

7. **Avocado**: Avocado is rich in healthy fats that provide long-lasting fuel for your body. Besides that, it has more potassium than a banana! It's great on toast, in smoothies, or even straight out of its skin with a bit of salt.

8. **Nuts (e.g., Almonds)**: These are convenient snack options loaded with protein and healthy fats. Almonds, specifically, also contain magnesium—a mineral that's pivotal for converting sugar into energy.

SUPERFOOD	KEY BENEFITS	HOW TO USE
Chia Seeds	Omega-3s, Protein, Fiber	Smoothies, Yogurt
Quinoa	Complete Protein, Iron, Magnesium	Salads, Breakfast
Spinach	Iron	Salads, Smoothies
Sweet Potatoes	Complex Carbs, Vitamin C & Manganese	Baked Trades
Blueberries	Antioxidants (Vitamin C & K)	Snacks, Desserts
Green Tea	Natural Energy Booster (Caffeine + L-theanine)	Teas
Avocado	Healthy Fats (Potassium)	Toasts, Smoothies
Nuts (e.g., Almonds)	Protein, Healthy Fats, Magnesium	Snacks, Salads

CHAPTER 4
Morning Boosts Breakfast

1. Berry Blast Smoothie Bowl

Preparation time: Ten mins

Cooking time: N/A

Servings: Two

Ingredients:

- One and a half cups mixed berries (strawberries, blueberries, raspberries)
- One ripe banana
- Half cup Greek yogurt
- Quarter cup almond milk
- One tbsp honey
- Two tbsp granola (for topping)
- Two tbsp sliced almonds (for topping)

Directions:

1. In a blender, mix berries, banana, yogurt, milk, and honey. Blend till smooth.
2. Pour it into two bowls. Top with granola and sliced almonds.

Tips: Use frozen berries for a thicker texture. Feel free to add a scoop of protein powder for extra nutrition.

Serving size: 1 bowl

Nutritional values (per serving): Calories: 210; Fat: 5g; Carbs: 38g; Protein: 6g; Sodium: 40mg; Sugar: 25g; Cholesterol: 0mg; Fiber: 7g

2. Mixed Nut and Seed Breakfast Bars

Preparation time: Fifteen mins

Cooking time: Twenty-five mins

Servings: Eight

Ingredients:

- One cup mixed nuts, chopped
- Half cup mixed seeds
- One cup rolled oats
- Quarter cup honey or maple syrup
- Quarter cup almond butter or peanut butter
- One tsp vanilla extract

Directions:

1. Warm up your oven to 350°F (175°C).
2. In your big container, mix chopped nuts, seeds, and rolled oats. In your small saucepan on low temp, dissolve honey and almond butter till smooth. Stir in vanilla.
3. Pour it on nut mixture and mix well to coat thoroughly. Press it evenly into your lined baking pan. Bake for twenty-five mins or till golden brown around the edges.
4. Cool it down before slicing into bars.

Tips: Add a handful of dried fruit for extra flavor.

Serving size: 1 bar

Nutritional values (per serving): Calories: 180; Fat: 12g; Carbs: 18g; Protein: 5g; Sodium: 30mg; Sugar: 9g; Cholesterol: 0mg; Fiber: 3g

3. Egg White and Veggie Omelette

Preparation time: Five mins

Cooking time: Ten mins

Servings: One

Ingredients:

- Three egg whites
- Quarter cup diced bell pepper
- Quarter cup diced onion
- Quarter cup chopped spinach
- One tbsp olive oil
- One tsp salt
- One tsp black pepper

Directions:

1. Warm up oil in your non-stick skillet on moderate temp. Sauté bell pepper, onion, and spinach to your skillet for about three mins till vegetables are tender.
2. Pour the egg whites, then flavor it using salt and black pepper. Cook for four to five mins, gently fold one half of the omelette over the other half, then cook for one minute.

Tips: You can add a pinch of your favorite herbs for extra flavor. Use a spatula to gently fold the omelette to avoid breaking.

Serving size: One omelette

Nutritional values (per serving): Calories: 120; Fat: 7g; Carbs: 6g; Protein: 9g; Sodium: 220mg; Sugar: 2g; Cholesterol: 0mg; Fiber: 2g

4. *Protein-Packed Breakfast Burrito*

Preparation time: Ten mins

Cooking time: Ten mins

Servings: Two

Ingredients:

- Three large eggs
- One cup black beans (canned)
- One-half cup shredded cheddar cheese
- Two whole wheat tortillas
- One avocado
- Two tbsp salsa
- One tsp olive oil

Directions:

Warm up your non-stick skillet on moderate temp and add olive oil. In your container, whisk the eggs and pour them into the skillet. Scramble till fully cooked.

While eggs are cooking, rinse and drain the black beans. Warm the tortillas in a separate pan or microwave.

Divide the scrambled eggs, black beans, cheese, and salsa between the tortillas. Slice the avocado and add it to each tortilla. Roll up each tortilla to form a burrito.

Tips: These burritos can be prepped ahead of time and reheated for a quick breakfast.

Serving size: 1 burrito

Nutritional values (per serving): Calories: 350; Fat: 18g; Carbs: 36g; Protein: 15g; Sodium: 500mg; Sugar: 2g; Cholesterol: 210mg; Fiber: 8g

5. *Coconut and Blueberry Overnight Oats*

Preparation time: Five mins + chilling time

Cooking time: N/A

Servings: Two

Ingredients:

- One cup old-fashioned oats
- One cup unsweetened coconut milk
- One-half cup fresh blueberries
- Two tbsp chia seeds
- Two tbsp shredded coconut
- One tbsp honey or maple syrup (optional)

Directions:

1. In your mason jar, mix oats, coconut milk, chia seeds, and shredded coconut. Mix well to ensure all ingredients are evenly distributed. Fold in fresh blueberries gently.
2. Cover, then refrigerate for four hours. Stir well before serving.

Tips: For added crunch, top with some nuts or granola before serving. Can be prepped for multiple days; lasts up to three days in the fridge.

Serving size: One cup

Nutritional values (per serving): Calories: 220; Fat: 11g; Carbs: 27g; Protein: 6g; Sodium: 65mg; Sugar: 10g; Cholesterol: 0mg; Fiber: 7g

6. *Almond Butter and Banana Toast*

Preparation time: Five mins

Cooking time: N/A

Servings: One

Ingredients:

- One slice bread, whole-grain, toasted
- Two tbsp almond butter
- Half banana, sliced
- Half tsp honey (optional)
- A pinch of cinnamon (optional)

Directions:

1. Spread the almond butter over the toasted bread. Arrange banana slices on top.
2. Drizzle with honey and sprinkle with cinnamon if desired.

Tips: Use a ripe banana for extra sweetness. Substitute almond butter with any nut or seed butter of your choice.

Serving size: 1 slice of toast

Nutritional values (per serving): Calories: 250; Fat: 14g; Carbs: 28g; Protein: 6g; Sodium: 120mg; Sugar: 9g; Cholesterol: 0mg; Fiber: 4g

7. *Pumpkin Spice Breakfast Muffins*

Preparation time: Ten mins

Cooking time: Twenty mins

Servings: Twelve muffins

Ingredients:

- One cup pumpkin puree, canned
- Two cups flour, whole wheat
- Half cup maple syrup
- Two tsp pumpkin pie spice
- Half cup olive oil or melted coconut oil
- Two large eggs
- One tsp baking soda
- Salt, as required

Directions:

1. Warm up your oven to 350°F (175°C).

2. In your big container, mix pumpkin puree, maple syrup, olive oil, and eggs.

3. In your separate container, whisk flour, pumpkin pie spice, baking soda, and salt. Combine it with pumpkin puree mixture till blended.

4. Divide it among your lined muffin cups, then bake for about twenty mins. Cool it down, then serve.

Tips: Add some nuts or dark chocolate chips for extra texture and flavor.

Serving size: 1 muffin

Nutritional values (per serving): Calories: 180; Fat: 8g; Carbs: 26g; Protein: 3g; Sodium: 160mg; Sugar: 10g; Cholesterol: 30mg; Fiber: 3g

8. *Apple and Cinnamon Quinoa Bowl*

Preparation time: Five mins

Cooking time: Fifteen mins

Servings: Two

Ingredients:

- One cup quinoa, washed
- Two cups water
- One apple, diced
- One tsp ground cinnamon
- Two tbsp honey
- One tsp vanilla extract
- Two tbsp chopped walnuts (optional)

Directions:

1. In your medium saucepan, mix quinoa and water. Let it boil on high temp. Adjust to low temp, cover, then simmer for fifteen mins till quinoa is tender.

2. Stir in diced apple, ground cinnamon, honey or maple syrup, and vanilla extract. Cook for an additional 2 mins till apples are slightly softened.

3. Serve warm, topped with chopped walnuts if desired.

Tips: Substitute honey with maple syrup for a vegan option. Add a splash of almond milk for a creamier texture.

Serving size: One bowl

Nutritional values (per serving): Calories: 320; Fat: 6g; Carbs: 65g; Protein: 7g; Sodium: 20mg; Sugar: 18g; Cholesterol: 0mg; Fiber: 7g

9. *Spinach and Mushroom Frittata*

Preparation time: Ten mins

Cooking time: Twenty mins

Servings: Four

Ingredients:

- Six large eggs
- One cup fresh spinach, chopped
- Half cup mushrooms, sliced
- Quarter cup milk (dairy or non-dairy)
- Quarter cup grated cheese (optional)
- One tbsp olive oil
- Salt & pepper, as required

Directions:

1. Warm up your oven to 350°F (175°C).
2. In your container, whisk eggs with milk, salt, and pepper till well combined. Warm up oil in an oven-safe skillet on moderate temp.
3. Add sliced mushrooms and cook till tender, about five mins. Add chopped spinach and sauté for another two mins till wilted.
4. Add egg mixture, tilting the pan to spread it evenly. Top with grated cheese if using. Transfer it to your oven, then bake for ten mins or till eggs are set.

Tips: Use non-stick cooking spray if you do not have an oven-safe skillet. Add other favorite veggies like bell peppers or onions.

Serving size: One slice

Nutritional values (per serving): Calories: 160; Fat: 11g; Carbs: 3g; Protein: 12g; Sodium: 210mg; Sugar: Less than one g; Cholesterol: 185mg; Fiber: Less than one g

10. *Tofu Scramble with Peppers and Onions*

Preparation time: Ten mins

Cooking time: Ten mins

Servings: Two

Ingredients:

- One tbsp olive oil
- One block firm tofu, drained and crumbled
- Half cup red onion, chopped
- Half cup bell pepper (any color), chopped
- One tsp turmeric powder
- Salt & pepper, as required
- Two tbsp nutritional yeast

Directions:

1. Warm up oil in your big pan on moderate temp. Add red onion and bell pepper, then sauté for five mins, till softened. Add the crumbled tofu to the pan, then mix well.
2. Add turmeric powder, salt, and pepper, then mix again. Cook for an additional 5 mins, stirring occasionally. Stir in the nutritional yeast at the end for an extra cheesy flavor.

Tips: Serve with a side of whole grain toast or avocado slices for added nutrients.

Serving size: One cup

Nutritional values (per serving): Calories: 180; Fat: 9g; Carbs: 8g; Protein: 15g; Sodium: 380mg; Sugar: 2g; Cholesterol: 0mg; Fiber: 3g

11.Savory Oatmeal with Avocado and Poached Egg

Preparation time: Five mins

Cooking time: Ten mins

Servings: Two

Ingredients:

- One cup rolled oats
- Two cups water or milk of choice
- One ripe avocado, sliced
- Two eggs, poached
- Salt & pepper, as required
- Half tsp chili flakes (optional)

Directions:

1. In a medium pot, let water boil. Add oats, adjust to low temp, then simmer for five mins till thickened.
2. While oats are cooking, poach the eggs in simmering water for about 3 mins. Divide the cooked oatmeal into two bowls.
3. Top each bowl with sliced avocado and one poached egg. Season with salt, pepper, and chili flakes if using.

Tips: Drizzle a bit of olive oil on top before serving for enhanced flavor.

Serving size: One bowl

Nutritional values (per serving): Calories: 350; Fat: 18g; Carbs: 40g; Protein: 12g; Sodium: 300mg; Sugar: 1g; Cholesterol: 190mg; Fiber: 10g

12. Cottage Cheese with Fresh Berries and Honey

Preparation time: Ten mins

Cooking time: N/A

Servings: Two

Ingredients:

- One cup cottage cheese
- One cup mixed fresh berries
- One tbsp honey
- One tsp chia seeds (optional)

Directions:

1. Split cottage cheese equally between two containers. Top each container with berries.
2. Drizzle half of the honey over each bowl. Sprinkle chia seeds on top if using.

Tips: Use organic and seasonal berries for the best flavor.

Serving size: Half cup

Nutritional values (per serving): Calories: 170; Fat: 3g; Carbs: 27g Protein: 12g; Sodium: 380mg; Sugar: 14g; Cholesterol: 10mg; Fiber: 4g

13. Matcha Green Tea Smoothie Bowl

Preparation time: Ten mins

Cooking time: N/A

Servings: Two

Ingredients:

- One cup unsweetened almond milk
- Two frozen bananas
- One tbsp matcha green tea powder
- Half cup baby spinach leaves
- Quarter cup granola

Directions:

1. Add almond milk into your blender. Add frozen bananas, matcha green tea powder, and baby spinach leaves.
2. Blend till smooth and creamy. Pour into bowls and top with granola.

Tips: For added texture, sprinkle coconut flakes or seeds on top. Use ripe bananas for extra sweetness without added sugar.

Serving size: One bowl

Nutritional values (per serving): Calories: 210; Fat: 4g; Carbs: 43g; Protein: 3g; Sodium: 150mg; Sugar: 19g; Cholesterol: 0mg; Fiber: 5g

14. Tomato and Basil Breakfast Tartine

Preparation time: Ten mins

Cooking time: N/A

Servings: Two

Ingredients:

- One ripe tomato, sliced thin
- Four slices of whole grain bread, toasted
- Two tbsp olive oil
- One halved garlic clove
- Four chopped basil leaves
- Salt & pepper, as required

Directions:

1. Rub toasted bread with the cut side of the garlic clove. Drizzle each slice with half a tablespoon of extra virgin olive oil.
2. Arrange tomato slices on each piece of toasted bread. Sprinkle chopped basil leaves over the tomatoes. Flavor it using salt and pepper.

Tips: You can add a sprinkle of grated Parmesan cheese for extra flavor.

Serving size: Two tartines

Nutritional values (per serving): Calories: 250; Fat: 14g; Carbs: 28g; Protein: 4g; Sodium: 200mg; Sugar: 3g; Cholesterol: 0g; Fiber: 5g

15. Buckwheat Pancakes with Fresh Fruit

Preparation time: Fifteen mins

Cooking time: Ten mins

Servings: Four

Ingredients:

- One cup buckwheat flour
- One cup almond milk
- One tbsp coconut oil, melted
- One tsp baking powder
- One tbsp honey or maple syrup
- Two cups fresh mixed berries
- Salt, as required

Directions:

1. In your container, whisk flour, baking powder, and salt. Add milk, melted coconut oil, and honey, then mix well till blended.
2. Warm up your non-stick skillet on moderate temp, then lightly grease with a bit of coconut oil.
3. Pour some batter onto your skillet. Cook each pancake for about two mins on each side or till bubbles form and they are golden brown.
4. Serve warm with fresh mixed berries on top.

Tips: You can add some yogurt on top for extra protein and creaminess.

Serving size: Two pancakes

Nutritional values (per serving): Calories: 200; Fat: 6g; Carbs: 32g; Protein: 5g; Sodium: 75mg; Sugar: 7g; Cholesterol: 0mg; Fiber: 6g

CHAPTER 5
Power-Packed Lunches

16. Quinoa and Avocado Power Bowl

Preparation time: Fifteen mins

Cooking time: Fifteen mins

Servings: Four

Ingredients:

- One cup quinoa, washed
- Two cups water
- One large avocado, diced
- One cup halved cherry tomatoes
- One cup spinach leaves
- One tbsp olive oil
- One tsp lemon juice
- Salt & pepper, as required

Directions:

1. In your medium saucepan, let quinoa and water boil. Adjust to low temp, cover, then simmer for fifteen mins. Fluff the quinoa, and cool it slightly.
2. In your big container, mix cooked quinoa, avocado, cherry tomatoes, and spinach leaves. Add olive oil, lemon juice, salt and pepper. Toss everything together till well mixed.

Tips: For added crunch, sprinkle some sunflower seeds or chopped nuts on top. You can substitute spinach with kale or arugula if preferred.

Serving size: One bowl

Nutritional values (per serving): Calories: 300; Fat: 14g; Carbs: 34g; Protein: 8g; Sodium: 120mg; Sugar: 2g; Cholesterol: 0mg; Fiber: 7g

17. Hummus and Veggie Whole Grain Wrap

Preparation time: Ten mins

Cooking time: N/A

Servings: Two

Ingredients:

- One cup hummus
- One cup shredded carrots
- One cup baby spinach leaves
- Half a cup sliced bell peppers
- Two whole grain wraps

Directions:

1. Spread half a cup hummus evenly over each whole grain wrap.
2. Layer half a cup shredded carrots, half a cup baby spinach, and a quarter cup sliced bell peppers on top of the hummus for each wrap.
3. Roll the wraps tightly and cut them in half if desired.

Tips: Add a sprinkle of your favorite herbs or spices for extra flavor.

Serving size: One wrap

Nutritional values (per serving): Calories: 250; Fat: 10g; Carbs: 32g; Protein: 8g; Sodium: 300mg; Sugar: 3g; Cholesterol: 0mg; Fiber: 7g

18. Chicken and Wild Rice Soup

Preparation time: Fifteen mins

Cooking time: Thirty mins

Servings: Four

Ingredients:

- One lb. cooked chicken breast, shredded
- Four cups chicken broth, low sodium
- One cup wild rice, cooked
- One cup carrots, diced
- One cup celery, diced
- Half tsp black pepper
- One tbsp olive oil

Directions:

1. Warm up oil in your big pot on moderate temp. Add carrots and celery, then sauté for five mins. Pour in broth, then let it boil.
2. Add the shredded chicken and cooked wild rice. Season with black pepper and let simmer for twenty-five mins.

Tips: Garnish with fresh parsley or thyme for added flavor.

Serving size: One bowl

Nutritional values (per serving): Calories: 200; Fat: 6g; Carbs: 18g; Protein: 20g; Sodium: 400mg; Sugar: 3g; Cholesterol: 40mg; Fiber: 2g

19. *Mediterranean Lentil Salad*

Preparation time: Ten mins

Cooking time: Twenty mins

Servings: Four

Ingredients:

- One cup green lentils, washed
- Two cups water
- One cup halved cherry tomatoes
- Half a cup cucumber, diced
- One fourth cup chopped red onion
- Two tbsp olive oil
- Juice of one lemon

Directions:

1. In your medium pot, let water boil. Add lentils, then simmer for twenty mins till tender. Strain, then cool it down.
2. In your big container, mix cooked lentils, cherry tomatoes, cucumber, and red onion. In your small container, whisk oil and lemon juice.
3. Pour dressing on your salad, then toss gently. Flavor it using salt and pepper.

Tips: Add chopped parsley or mint for extra flavor.

Serving size: One cup

Nutritional values (per serving): Calories: 210; Fat: 7g; Carbs: 28g; Protein: 9g; Sodium: 20mg; Sugar: 6g; Cholesterol: 0mg; Fiber: 8g

20. Grilled Chicken and Pesto Panini

Preparation time: Ten mins

Cooking time: Ten mins

Servings: Two

Ingredients:

- One half lb. boneless, skinless chicken breast
- Two tbsp pesto sauce
- One fourth cup roasted red bell peppers, sliced
- Two slices of whole-grain bread
- One tbsp olive oil or cooking spray

Directions:

1. Warm up your grill pan on moderate-high temp. Flavor chicken breast using salt and pepper. Grill the chicken for about five mins on each side till fully cooked.
2. Let the chicken rest for a few mins, then slice thinly. On one slice of bread, spread one tbsp pesto sauce. Layer sliced chicken and roasted red bell peppers on top.
3. Spread another tbsp pesto sauce on the second bread slice and place it on top to form a sandwich. Lightly brush or spray both sides of the sandwich with olive oil.
4. Put sandwich on the grill pan and press down with another heavy skillet or a panini press for two-three mins per side till golden brown.

Tips: You can add a slice of mozzarella cheese for an extra creamy texture. Use leftover grilled chicken to save time.

Serving size: One sandwich

Nutritional values (per serving): Calories: 350; Fat: 14g; Carbs: 30g; Protein: 28g; Sodium: 590mg; Sugar: 4g; Cholesterol: 55mg; Fiber: 4g

21. Butternut Squash and Lentil Soup

Preparation time: Fifteen mins

Cooking time: Thirty mins

Servings: Four

Ingredients:

- Two cups diced butternut squash
- One cup red lentils, rinsed
- Four cups vegetable broth
- One medium onion, chopped
- Two cloves garlic, minced
- One tsp ground cumin
- One tbsp olive oil
- Salt & pepper, as required

Directions:

1. In a large pot, warm up oil on moderate temp. Add onion and garlic, sauté till translucent.
2. Add diced butternut squash and ground cumin; cook for an additional three mins, stirring occasionally.
3. Add lentils and broth, let it boil, then adjust to simmer for twenty-five mins or till lentils and squash are tender.
4. Purée the soup using your immersion blender till smooth or leave it chunky if preferred. Flavor it using salt and pepper.

Tips: For added flavor, garnish with cilantro or some plain yogurt.

Serving size: One cup

Nutritional values (per serving): Calories: 190; Fat: 4g; Carbs: 32g; Protein: 8g; Sodium: 500mg; Sugar: 5g; Cholesterol: 0mg; Fiber: 8g

22. Grilled Chicken and Mango Salad

Preparation time: Ten mins

Cooking time: Fifteen mins

Servings: Four

Ingredients:

- One lb. chicken breast, grilled and sliced
- Two cups mixed greens (spinach, arugula, etc.)
- One ripe mango, peeled and diced

- Half cup halved cherry tomatoes
- One cucumber, sliced
- One tbsp olive oil
- Two tbsp lime juice
- Salt & pepper, as required

Directions:

1. Warm up your grill to moderate-high temp. Flavor chicken breasts using salt and pepper.
2. Grill the chicken breasts for six to seven mins on each side. Cool it down before slicing.
3. In your big container, combine mixed greens, diced mango, cherry tomatoes, and cucumber slices. Arrange grilled chicken slices on top of the salad.
4. In your small container, whisk oil and lime juice. Drizzle on your salad just before serving.

Tips: For a bit of crunch, add some chopped nuts like almonds or walnuts.

Serving size: One and a half cups

Nutritional values (per serving): Calories: 250; Fat: 9g; Carbs: 22g; Protein: 25g; Sodium: 400mg; Sugar: 14g; Cholesterol: 50mg; Fiber: 4g

23. Turkey and Avocado Club Wrap

Preparation time: Ten mins

Cooking time: N/A

Servings: Four

Ingredients:

- Four whole-wheat tortillas
- Eight oz. sliced turkey breast
- One large avocado, sliced
- One cup shredded lettuce
- Half cup diced tomatoes
- Two tbsp mayonnaise
- Half tsp powdered garlic
- Salt & pepper, as required

Directions:

1. In your small container, mix mayonnaise with powdered garlic. Lay out each tortilla flat on your clean surface.
2. Spread some garlic mayo mixture on each tortilla. Layer the turkey slices evenly on each tortilla. Add avocado slices, shredded lettuce, and diced tomatoes on top of the turkey.
3. Flavor it using salt and pepper. Roll up each tortilla tightly into a wrap.

Tips: You can add slices of cheese for extra flavor. For an added kick, include some thinly sliced red onions or jalapeños.

Serving size: One wrap

Nutritional values (per serving): Calories: 350; Fat: 18g; Carbs: 27g; Protein: 22g; Sodium: 650mg; Sugar: 2g; Cholesterol: 35mg; Fiber: 6g

24. *Vegetable and Quinoa Stew*

Preparation time: Ten mins

Cooking time: Twenty-five mins

Servings: Four

Ingredients:

- One cup quinoa, washed
- Two cups vegetable broth
- One cup diced carrots
- One cup diced zucchini
- One can (15 oz.) diced tomatoes, unstrained
- One tsp olive oil
- Two tsp powdered garlic
- One tsp ground cumin
- Salt & pepper, as required

Directions:

1. Warm up oil in your big pot on moderate temp. Add carrots and cook for 5 mins till tender. Mix in powdered garlic, cumin, salt, and pepper.
2. Add quinoa, broth, zucchini, and tomatoes. Let it boil, then simmer for twenty mins till quinoa is cooked and vegetables are tender.

Tips: For extra flavor, add a splash of lemon juice before serving.

Serving size: 1 bowl

Nutritional values (per serving): Calories: 180; Fat: 4g; Carbs: 32g; Protein: 6g; Sodium: 400mg; Sugar: 5g; Cholesterol: 0mg; Fiber: 6g

25. Sweet Potato and Black Bean Buddha Bowl

Preparation time: Ten mins

Cooking time: Twenty mins

Servings: Four

Ingredients:

- Two big sweet potatoes, peeled & cubed
- Two tbsp olive oil
- One can (15 oz.) black beans, strained & washed
- Two cups cooked brown rice
- One avocado, sliced
- One tsp chili powder
- Salt & pepper, as required

Directions:

1. Warm up your oven to 400°F (200°C). Mix sweet potatoes, oil, chili powder, salt, and pepper on your baking sheet. Roast in the oven for about 20 mins till tender.
2. In your container, add a layer of cooked brown rice or quinoa. Top with roasted sweet potatoes, black beans, and avocado slices.

Tips: Squeeze fresh lime juice over the bowl for an extra zesty flavor. Add a handful of greens like spinach or kale for more nutrients.

Serving size: 1 bowl

Nutritional values (per serving): Calories: 350; Fat: 14g; Carbs: 55g; Protein: 9g; Sodium: 300mg; Sugar: 6g; Cholesterol: 0mg; Fiber: 12g

26. Tuna and Spinach Whole Wheat Sandwich

Preparation time: Fifteen mins

Cooking time: N/A

Servings: Two

Ingredients:

- One can of tuna in water, strained
- Two cups fresh spinach leaves
- Four slices whole wheat bread
- Two tbsp mayonnaise, reduced-fat
- One tbsp Dijon mustard
- One tsp lemon juice
- Salt & pepper, as required

Directions:

1. In your medium container, mix tuna, mayonnaise, mustard, and lemon juice. Flavor it using salt and pepper. Spread it onto two slices of whole wheat bread.
2. Top with fresh spinach leaves and then cover with the remaining bread slices. Serve.

Tips: Add a slice of tomato or avocado for extra flavor. Use gluten-free bread for a gluten-free option.

Serving size: One sandwich

Nutritional values (per serving): Calories: 300; Fat: 8g; Carbs: 30g; Protein: 25g; Sodium: 600mg; Sugar: 3g; Cholesterol: 30mg; Fiber: 5g

27. Hearty Minestrone Soup

Preparation time: Ten mins

Cooking time: Twenty-five mins

Servings: Four

Ingredients:

- One tbsp olive oil
- One cup onion, chopped
- Two minced cloves garlic
- Two cups vegetable broth
- One can diced tomatoes (fourteen oz.), undrained
- One cup chopped zucchini
- One cup cooked kidney beans (canned works well)
- One tsp dried basil

Directions:

1. Warm up oil in your big pot on moderate temp. Add onion and garlic, sauté for three mins till softened.
2. Pour in broth and tomatoes, including their liquid. Add zucchini, then let it boil. Cover, then simmer for fifteen mins till vegetables are tender.
3. Stir in kidney beans and dried basil, cook for another five to ten mins. Flavor it using salt and pepper before serving.

Tips: Add a handful of fresh spinach or kale at the end for some extra nutrients. Serve with crusty whole grain bread.

Serving size: One cup

Nutritional values (per serving): Calories: 150; Fat: 4g; Carbs: 23g; Protein: 4g; Sodium: 500mg; Sugar: 8g; Cholesterol: 0mg; Fiber: 6g

28. *Asian-Inspired Salmon Poke Bowl*

Preparation time: Fifteen mins

Cooking time: N/A

Servings: Four

Ingredients:

- One lb. fresh sushi-grade salmon, diced
- Two cups brown rice, cooked
- One avocado, sliced
- One cup edamame, shelled
- One cucumber, thinly sliced
- Two tbsp soy sauce, low-sodium
- One tbsp rice vinegar
- One tsp sesame oil

Directions:

1. In your medium container, mix diced salmon, soy sauce, rice vinegar, and sesame oil. Gently toss to coat.
2. Put brown rice among four bowls. Top each bowl with marinated salmon, avocado slices, edamame, and cucumber slices.

3. Sprinkle with sesame seeds if desired. Serve immediately.

Tips: Ensure the salmon is extremely fresh or sushi-grade to avoid any issues.

Serving size: 1 bowl

Nutritional values (per serving): Calories: 350; Fat: 18g; Carbs: 28g; Protein: 24g; Sodium: 300mg; Sugar: 3g; Cholesterol: 45mg; Fiber: 6g

29. *Roasted Red Pepper and Hummus Wrap*

Preparation time: Ten mins

Cooking time: N/A

Servings: Four

Ingredients:

- Two cups roasted red peppers (jarred or homemade)
- One cup hummus
- Four tortillas, whole-wheat
- One cup baby spinach leaves
- Half cup shredded carrots

Directions:

1. Lay out tortillas on your clean surface. Spread about a quarter cup hummus onto each tortilla.
2. Layer on roasted red peppers evenly among the four tortillas. Add baby spinach leaves and shredded carrots on top of the peppers.
3. Roll up each tortilla tightly into a wrap. Serve.

Tips: For variation, try adding sliced avocado or cucumbers for extra crunch. You can also swap out whole-wheat tortillas for low-carb wraps if preferred.

Serving size: One wrap

Nutritional values (per serving): Calories: 280; Fat: 10g; Carbs: 36g; Protein: 8g; Sodium: 400mg; Sugar: 5g; Cholesterol: 0mg; Fiber: 8g

30. *Greek Salad with Quinoa and Feta*

Preparation time: Ten mins

Cooking time: Fifteen mins

Servings: Four

Ingredients:

- One cup quinoa, washed
- Two cups water
- One cucumber, diced
- One cup halved cherry tomatoes
- Half cup feta cheese, crumbled
- Quarter cup kalamata olives, pitted and sliced
- Two tbsp olive oil
- One tbsp lemon juice

Directions:

1. In your medium saucepan, let water boil. Add quinoa, adjust to low temp, cover, then simmer for fifteen mins till water is absorbed. Allow quinoa to cool slightly.
2. In your big container, combine quinoa with cucumber, cherry tomatoes, feta cheese, and kalamata olives. Add oil and lemon juice, then toss well.

Tips: For extra freshness, add some chopped fresh mint or parsley.

Serving size: One cup

Nutritional values (per serving): Calories: 220; Fat: 10g; Carbs: 25g; Protein: 8g; Sodium: 400mg; Sugar: 3g; Cholesterol: 15mg; Fiber: 4g

CHAPTER 6

Wind Down with Wholesome Dinners

31.Sweet Potato and Kale Stew

Preparation time: Ten mins

Cooking time: Twenty-five mins

Servings: Four

Ingredients:

- Two cups sweet potatoes, peeled and cubed
- One cup kale, chopped
- One can (15 oz.) diced tomatoes
- Two cups vegetable broth
- One tbsp olive oil
- One onion, chopped
- Two minced cloves garlic
- One tsp dried thyme

Directions:

1. Warm up oil in your big pot on moderate temp. Put onion and garlic, then sauté till translucent.
2. Mix in sweet potatoes, then cook for five mins. Add diced tomatoes, vegetable broth, and thyme.
3. Let it boil, then simmer for fifteen mins. Mix in kale, then cook for five mins. Flavor it using salt and pepper.

Tips: For added flavor, sprinkle some red pepper flakes or add a dash of smoked paprika.

Serving size: One cup

Nutritional values (per serving): Calories: 150; Fat: 5g; Carbs: 25g; Protein: 3g; Sodium: 300mg; Sugar: 6g; Cholesterol: 0mg; Fiber: 4g

32. Turkey and Spinach Stuffed Shells

Preparation time: Twenty mins

Cooking time: Twenty-five mins

Servings: Four

Ingredients:

- One lb. ground turkey
- Two cups fresh spinach, chopped
- One cup ricotta cheese
- One cup marinara sauce
- Twelve jumbo pasta shells, cooked and drained
- One tsp powdered garlic
- One tsp Italian seasoning

Directions:

1. Warm up your oven to 375°F (190°C).
2. In your medium skillet, cook ground turkey till browned and fully cooked. Add spinach, then cook for two mins till wilted.
3. In your big container, mix turkey, spinach, ricotta cheese, powdered garlic, and Italian seasoning. Fill each cooked pasta shell with it.
4. Spread some marinara sauce on your baking dish. Arrange stuffed shells in your baking dish, then pour the remaining marinara sauce over them.
5. Cover with aluminum foil, then bake for twenty-five mins. Serve hot.

Tips: Serve with a side salad for a complete meal.

Serving size: 3 stuffed shells

Nutritional values (per serving): Calories: 320; Fat: 11g; Carbs: 28g; Protein: 28g; Sodium: 580mg; Sugar: 4g; Cholesterol: 70mg; Fiber: 3g

33. Moroccan-Spiced Vegetable Tagine

Preparation time: Fifteen mins

Cooking time: Thirty mins

Servings: Four

Ingredients:

- One tbsp olive oil
- One large chopped onion
- Two cups carrots, peeled and sliced
- Two cups zucchini, chopped
- One can (14 oz.) chickpeas, drained and rinsed
- One cup vegetable broth
- One tbsp ras el hanout spice blend
- One cup dried apricots, chopped

Directions:

1. Warm up oil in your big pot on moderate temp. Add onion, then sauté for five 5 mins till translucent.
2. Add carrots and zucchini, then cook for another five mins. Mix in chickpeas, broth, ras el hanout spice blend, and dried apricots.
3. Let it boil, then simmer for twenty mins. Serve hot over cooked couscous or quinoa.

Tips: Garnish with fresh cilantro for added flavor.

Serving size: One cup

Nutritional values (per serving): Calories: 280; Fat: 6g; Carbs: 50g; Protein: 8g; Sodium: 420mg; Sugar: 18g; Cholesterol: 0mg; Fiber: 10g

34. Teriyaki Chicken with Steamed Veggies

Preparation time: Ten mins

Cooking time: Twenty mins

Servings: Four

Ingredients:

- One lb. chicken breast, cut into strips
- Half cup teriyaki sauce
- One cup broccoli florets
- One cup carrot slices
- One cup bell pepper strips
- Two tbsp olive oil

- One tsp sesame seeds (optional)

Directions:

1. In your container, marinate the chicken strips in teriyaki sauce for at least 10 mins. Warm up oil in a pan on moderate temp.
2. Add marinated chicken to the pan and cook for about 10 mins or till fully cooked. While the chicken is cooking, steam the broccoli, carrots, and bell peppers for about 5-7 mins till tender.
3. Mix cooked chicken and steamed veggies. Stir well to coat evenly with any remaining teriyaki sauce. Sprinkle sesame seeds on top if desired.

Tips: Serve with brown rice or quinoa for a complete meal. Use fresh vegetables for better taste and nutrition.

Serving size: 1 cup

Nutritional values (per serving): Calories: 250; Fat: 9g; Carbs: 12g; Protein: 28g; Sodium: 750mg; Sugar: 7g; Cholesterol: 65mg; Fiber: 3g

35. Baked Zucchini Lasagna

Preparation time: Fifteen mins

Cooking time: Thirty mins

Servings: Four

Ingredients:

- Two big zucchinis, thinly sliced lengthwise
- One cup marinara sauce
- Half cup ricotta cheese
- Half cup mozzarella cheese, shredded
- Quarter cup Parmesan cheese, grated
- One lb. lean ground turkey
- One tbsp olive oil
- Salt & pepper, as required

Directions:

1. Warm up your oven to 375°F (190°C).

2. In your pan, warm up oil on moderate temp, then cook ground turkey till browned. Flavor turkey using salt and pepper, then mix in marinara sauce till well combined.
3. In a baking dish, layer zucchini slices at the bottom followed by a layer of turkey mixture.
4. Spread dollops of ricotta cheese over the meat mixture, then sprinkle mozzarella and Parmesan cheeses.
5. Repeat layers, ending with a topping of mozzarella and Parmesan cheeses. Bake for thirty mins till cheese is melted and golden brown.

Tips: Pat zucchini slices dry with paper towels to reduce water content before layering. Let lasagna rest for a few mins before serving for easier slicing.

Serving size: One slice

Nutritional values (per serving): Calories: 320; Fat: 18g; Carbs: 10g; Protein: 40g; Sodium: 600mg; Sugar: 6g; Cholesterol: 90mg; Fiber: 3g

36. Vegan Thai Green Curry with Tofu

Preparation time: Fifteen mins

Cooking time: Twenty mins

Servings: Four

Ingredients:

- One tbsp coconut oil
- One lb. firm tofu, cubed
- Two cups coconut milk
- Two tbsp green curry paste
- One cup bell peppers, sliced
- One cup carrots, sliced
- One cup snap peas
- Two tbsp soy sauce

Directions:

1. Warm up oil in your big pan on moderate temp. Add cubed tofu and cook for five to seven mins till golden brown on all sides.
2. Mix in green curry paste, then cook for one minute. Add coconut milk and soy sauce, stirring well to combine.

3. Add the bell peppers, carrots, and snap peas. Simmer for ten mins till vegetables are tender. Serve hot with rice or noodles.

Tips: For added flavor, garnish with fresh basil or cilantro before serving.

Serving size: One cup

Nutritional values (per serving): Calories: 290; Fat: 20g; Carbs: 20g; Protein: 10g; Sodium: 600mg; Sugar: 5g; Cholesterol: 0mg; Fiber: 4g

37. Black Bean and Sweet Potato Enchiladas

Preparation time: Fifteen mins

Cooking time: Twenty-five mins

Servings: Four

Ingredients:

- One tbsp olive oil
- One lb. sweet potatoes, peeled & diced
- One cup black beans, strained & washed
- One tbsp chili powder
- Eight whole wheat tortillas
- One cup enchilada sauce
- One cup cheddar cheese, shredded

Directions:

1. Warm up your oven to 375°F (190°C). Warm up oil in your big skillet on moderate temp. Add diced sweet potatoes, then cook for ten mins till tender.
2. Add black beans and chili powder to the skillet, stirring to combine. Place the sweet potato and black bean mixture evenly in the center of each tortilla.
3. Roll up tortillas, then put them seam side down in your baking dish. Add enchilada sauce on your rolled tortillas, then sprinkle with shredded cheddar cheese.
4. Bake for fifteen mins or till cheese is melted and bubbly.

Tips: Serve with a side of fresh salsa or guacamole for added flavor.

Serving size: Two enchiladas

Nutritional values (per serving): Calories: 360; Fat: 14g; Carbs: 48g; Protein: 13g; Sodium: 710mg; Sugar: 6g; Cholesterol: 25mg; Fiber: 8g

38. Spicy Chicken and Veggie Skewers

Preparation time: Fifteen mins

Cooking time: Twenty mins

Servings: Four

Ingredients:

- One lb. chicken breast cubes
- One red bell pepper, cut into chunks
- One zucchini, sliced into rounds
- Two tbsp olive oil
- One tbsp chili powder
- Two tsp powdered garlic
- Salt & pepper, as required

Directions:

1. Warm up your grill to moderate-high temp.
2. In your big container, toss chicken cubes, bell pepper chunks, and zucchini slices with olive oil, chili powder, powdered garlic, salt, and pepper.
3. Thread chicken and vegetables alternately onto skewers. Grill them for ten mins on each side or till chicken is cooked through.

Tips: Soak wooden skewers in water for thirty mins before grilling to prevent them from burning.

Serving size: Two skewers

Nutritional values (per serving): Calories: 270; Fat: 12g; Carbs: 8g; Protein: 30g; Sodium: 160mg; Sugar: 3g; Cholesterol: 75mg; Fiber: 2g

39. Rosemary Roasted Chicken with Root Vegetables

Preparation time: Fifteen mins

Cooking time: Fifty mins

Servings: Four

Ingredients:

- Three lbs. chicken thighs, bone-in
- Two cups baby potatoes, halved

- Two cups carrots, chopped
- Two tbsp olive oil
- One tbsp fresh rosemary, chopped
- Two tsp powdered garlic
- Salt & pepper, as required

Directions:

1. Warm up your oven to 400°F (200°C). Put chicken thighs, baby potatoes, and carrots in your big baking dish.
2. Add olive oil, rosemary, powdered garlic, salt, and pepper. Toss everything together till well coated.
3. Arrange chicken skin side up on top of vegetables. Roast in preheated oven for fifty mins or till chicken is cooked.

Tips: For crispier skin, you can broil the chicken for an additional Three to Five mins at the end of cooking.

Serving size: One chicken thigh with One cup vegetables

Nutritional values (per serving): Calories: 450; Fat: 25g; Carbs: 22g; Protein: 30g; Sodium: 400mg; Sugar: 6g; Cholesterol: 100mg; Fiber: 5g

40. Cauliflower Mac and Cheese

Preparation time: Ten mins

Cooking time: Twenty mins

Servings: Four

Ingredients:

- One medium cauliflower head, chopped into small florets
- Two cups cheddar cheese, shredded
- One cup almond milk, unsweetened
- One tbsp Dijon mustard
- One tsp powdered garlic
- One tsp powdered onion
- Salt & pepper, as required

Directions:

1. Warm up your oven to 375°F (190°C).   Steam the cauliflower florets till tender, about seven mins. Strain, then put aside.
2. In your saucepan on moderate temp, mix almond milk, cheddar cheese, mustard, powdered garlic, powdered onion, salt, and pepper till the cheese melts and forms a creamy sauce.
3. Add the steamed cauliflower to the cheese sauce, then mix well. Transfer it to your baking dish and bake for ten mins till bubbly. Let it cool slightly before serving.

Tips: For extra flavor, add a dash of paprika or your favorite herbs. This dish can be made ahead of time; simply reheat before serving.

Serving size: 1 cup

Nutritional values (per serving): Calories: 200; Fat: 15g; Carbs: 8g; Protein: 10g; Sodium: 300mg; Sugar: 2g; Cholesterol: 40mg; Fiber: 3g

41. Vegan Cauliflower Tacos

Preparation time: Fifteen mins

Cooking time: Twenty mins

Servings: Four

Ingredients:

- One medium cauliflower head, chopped into small florets
- Two tbsp olive oil
- One tbsp chili powder
- One tsp cumin
- Half tsp powdered garlic
- Half tsp smoked paprika
- Salt & pepper, as required
- Eight small corn tortillas, warmed

Directions:

1. Warm up your oven to 400°F (200°C).
2. In your container, mix cauliflower, oil, chili powder, cumin, powdered garlic, paprika, salt, and pepper.
3. Spread the seasoned cauliflower onto your lined baking sheet. Roast for twenty mins till crispy, stirring halfway through.

4. Assemble the tacos by placing roasted cauliflower on each tortilla.

Tips: Top with avocado slices, lime juice, fresh cilantro, or your favorite salsa for extra flavor. For spicier tacos, add a pinch of cayenne pepper to the seasoning mix.

Serving size: Two tacos

Nutritional values (per serving): Calories: 250; Fat: 12g; Carbs: 30g; Protein: 5g; Sodium: 350mg; Sugar: 3g; Cholesterol: 0mg; Fiber: 6g

42. Baked Cod with Tomato Basil Sauce

Preparation time: Fifteen mins

Cooking time: Twenty mins

Servings: Four

Ingredients:

- Four cod fillets (about one lb. total)
- One cup halved cherry tomatoes
- One tbsp olive oil
- Five cloves garlic, minced
- One tsp dried basil
- Half tsp sea salt
- Quarter tsp black pepper

Directions:

1. Warm up your oven to 400°F (200°C). Put cod fillets in your baking dish and sprinkle with sea salt and black pepper.
2. In your container, mix cherry tomatoes, minced garlic, olive oil, and dried basil. Spread the tomato mixture on cod fillets.
3. Bake for twenty mins or till the fish flakes easily.

Tips: Add a splash of lemon juice before serving for extra zest.

Serving size: One fillet

Nutritional values (per serving): Calories: 150; Fat: 5g; Carbs: 5g; Protein: 22g; Sodium: 350mg; Sugar: 2g; Cholesterol: 50mg; Fiber: 1g

43. Healthy Turkey Meatloaf

Preparation time: Fifteen mins

Cooking time: Forty-five mins

Servings: Six

Ingredients:

- One lb. ground turkey breast
- Half cup quick oats
- One egg, beaten
- Half cup finely chopped onion
- Two cloves garlic, minced
- One cup tomato sauce, divided
- One tsp dried oregano
- Half tsp sea salt
- Quarter tsp black pepper

Directions:

1. Warm up your oven to 375°F (190°C).
2. In your big container, mix ground turkey, quick oats, beaten egg, chopped onion, minced garlic, half cup tomato sauce, dried oregano, sea salt, and pepper.
3. Mix till well, then form into a loaf shape. Place the meatloaf in a baking dish, then top with remaining tomato sauce.
4. Bake for forty-five mins or till cooked through and juices run clear.

Tips: Let meatloaf rest for five mins before slicing for best results. Serve with steamed vegetables or mashed sweet potatoes for a balanced meal.

Serving size: One slice (1/6 of loaf)

Nutritional values (per serving): Calories: 200; Fat: 5g; Carbs: 12g; Protein: 28g; Sodium: 450mg; Sugar: 4g; Cholesterol: 70mg; Fiber: 2g

44. Mushroom and Tofu Stir-Fry

Preparation time: Fifteen mins

Cooking time: Fifteen mins

Servings: Four

Ingredients:

- Two tbsp vegetable oil
- One lb. firm tofu, cubed
- Two cups mushrooms, sliced
- One cup bell peppers, sliced
- Two tbsp soy sauce
- One tsp powdered garlic
- One tsp ginger powder
- Two green onions, chopped

Directions:

1. Warm up one tbsp oil in your big skillet on moderate-high temp. Add tofu cubes, then cook for five to seven mins till golden brown. Remove, then put aside.
2. In your same skillet, add the remaining oil and sauté the mushrooms and bell peppers for five mins till tender.
3. Return the tofu to the skillet, add soy sauce, powdered garlic, and ginger powder. Stir well to combine.
4. Cook for an additional three mins to blend flavors. Garnish with chopped green onions before serving.

Tips: Serve with a side of steamed rice or quinoa for a more filling meal.

Serving size: One cup

Nutritional values (per serving): Calories: 190; Fat: 9g; Carbs: 13g; Protein: 13g; Sodium: 550mg; Sugar: 4g; Cholesterol: 0mg; Fiber: 3g

45. Maple-Glazed Pork Chops with Sweet Potatoes

Preparation time: Five mins

Cooking time: Twenty-five mins

Servings: Four

Ingredients:

- Four pork chops (about one lb.)
- Two cups sweet potatoes, peeled & diced

- Quarter cup maple syrup
- Two tbsp Dijon mustard
- One tbsp olive oil
- One tsp powdered garlic
- Half tsp salt
- Half tsp black pepper

Directions:

1. Warm up your oven to 400°F (200°C).
2. In your small container, whisk maple syrup, mustard, powdered garlic, salt, and black pepper. Toss sweet potatoes with oil in your baking dish.
3. Put pork chops on top of sweet potatoes and brush maple syrup mixture over both pork chops and sweet potatoes.
4. Bake in preheated oven for twenty-five mins or till pork chops are thoroughly cooked (internal temperature should reach 145°F) and sweet potatoes are tender.

Tips: Let the pork chops rest for three mins before serving to retain juiciness.

Serving size: One pork chop with half cup sweet potatoes

Nutritional values (per serving): Calories: 350; Fat: 11g; Carbs: 38g; Protein: 23g; Sodium: 600mg; Sugar: 19g; Cholesterol: 70mg; Fiber: 4g

CHAPTER 7
Energy-Boosting Snacks

46. *Roasted Almonds with Sea Salt*

Preparation time: Five mins

Cooking time: Fifteen mins

Servings: Four

Ingredients:

- Two cups raw almonds
- One tbsp olive oil
- One tsp sea salt

Directions:

1. Warm up your oven to 350°F (175°C).
2. In your container, mix almonds and olive oil, then spread them on your baking sheet.
3. Roast for fifteen mins, stirring once halfway through. Remove, then sprinkle with sea salt while still warm.

Tips: Store roasted almonds in an airtight container to keep them fresh longer. Add a pinch of smoked paprika for an extra flavor kick.

Serving size: One-quarter cup

Nutritional values (per serving): Calories: 206; Fat: 18g; Carbs: 8g; Protein: 7g; Sodium: 150mg; Sugar: 1g; Cholesterol: 0mg; Fiber: 4g

47. *Mini Caprese Skewers*

Preparation time: Ten mins

Cooking time: N/A

Servings: Four

Ingredients:

- One cup halved cherry tomatoes
- One cup small mozzarella balls (bocconcini)
- One cup basil leaves
- Two tbsp balsamic glaze
- One tbsp olive oil
- Salt & pepper, as required

Directions:

1. Thread one cherry tomato half, one mozzarella ball, and one basil leaf onto small skewers or toothpicks.
2. Arrange them on your serving plate. Drizzle with olive oil and balsamic glaze. Flavor it using salt and pepper.

Tips: Use colored cherry tomatoes for a vibrant presentation. Serve immediately for the freshest taste.

Serving size: Three skewers

Nutritional values (per serving): Calories: 112; Fat: 9g; Carbs: 4g; Protein: 6g; Sodium: 220mg; Sugar: 3g; Cholesterol: 20mg; Fiber: 1g

48. Blueberry and Oat Energy Bars

Preparation time: Ten mins

Cooking time: Twenty mins

Servings: Eight

Ingredients:

- One and a half cups rolled oats
- Half cup almond butter
- One quarter cup honey
- One quarter cup dried blueberries
- Two tbsp chia seeds
- One tsp vanilla extract

Directions:

1. Warm up your oven to 350°F (175°C).

2. In your container, mix almond butter, honey, and vanilla extract. Add rolled oats, dried blueberries, and chia seeds to the mixture.

3. Spread it into your baking dish, pressing it down firmly. Bake for about twenty mins or till edges are golden brown. Cool it down before slicing into bars.

Tips: Use fresh blueberries for a different texture. Substitute almond butter with peanut butter if desired.

Serving size: 1 bar

Nutritional values (per serving): Calories: 150; Fat: 9g; Carbs: 18g; Protein: 4g; Sodium: 40mg; Sugar: 8g; Cholesterol: 0mg; Fiber: 3g

49. Cucumber and Hummus Roll-Ups

Preparation time: Ten mins

Cooking time: N/A

Servings: Four

Ingredients:

- Two large cucumbers
- One cup hummus
- One quarter cup chopped bell peppers
- Two tbsp chopped fresh parsley
- Two tbsp chopped olives (optional)

Directions:

1. Using a vegetable peeler or mandoline slicer, slice cucumbers lengthwise into thin strips. Spread some hummus on each cucumber strip.

2. Sprinkle chopped bell peppers, parsley, and olives over the hummus-covered strips. Roll up each strip tightly, then secure with a toothpick if necessary.

Tips: Add a squeeze of lemon juice for extra zest. Opt for flavored hummus to add variety.

Serving size: 1 roll-up

Nutritional values (per serving): Calories: 50; Fat: 2g; Carbs: 6g; Protein: 2g; Sodium: 120mg; Sugar: 1g; Cholesterol: 0mg; Fiber: 1g

50.Spiced Pumpkin Seeds

Preparation time: Ten mins

Cooking time: Twenty mins

Servings: Four

Ingredients:

- Two cups pumpkin seeds
- Two tbsp olive oil
- One tbsp chili powder
- One tsp powdered garlic
- One tsp ground cumin
- Half tsp paprika
- Salt to taste

Directions:

1. Warm up your oven to 350°F (175°C).
2. In your big container, mix pumpkin seeds, oil, chili powder, powdered garlic, cumin, paprika, and salt.
3. Spread seasoned pumpkin seeds on your baking sheet. Bake for twenty mins, stirring occasionally, till seeds are toasted.

Tips: Add a pinch of cayenne pepper if you like extra heat.

Serving size: Half cup

Nutritional values (per serving): Calories: 200; Fat: 16g; Carbs: 8g; Protein: 7g; Sodium: 150mg; Sugar: 0g; Cholesterol: 0mg; Fiber: 3g

51.Carrot and Apple Slaw

Preparation time: Fifteen mins

Cooking time: N/A

Servings: Four

Ingredients:

- Two cups shredded carrots
- Two cups shredded apple (such as Granny Smith)
- Juice of one lemon
- Quarter cup plain Greek yogurt
- One tbsp honey
- Salt to taste
- Pepper to taste

Directions:

1. In your big container, mix shredded carrots and apples.
2. In your separate small container, mix lemon juice, Greek yogurt, honey, salt, and pepper.
3. Pour it over your carrot and apple mixture and toss till well combined. Refrigerate for at least half an hour, then serve.

Tips: Use a mandoline for easy shredding.

Serving size: 1 cup

Nutritional values (per serving): Calories: 90; Fat: 2g; Carbs: 18g; Protein: 3g; Sodium: 60mg; Sugar: 12g; Cholesterol: 0mg; Fiber: 3g

52. *Pumpkin Seed and Cranberry Bars*

Preparation time: Ten mins

Cooking time: Twenty mins

Servings: Eight

Ingredients:

- One cup rolled oats
- Half cup pumpkin seeds
- Half cup dried cranberries
- One-third cup honey
- One-third cup almond butter
- One tsp vanilla extract

Directions:

1. Warm up your oven to 350°F (175°C).
2. In your big container, mix oats, pumpkin seeds, and dried cranberries.

3. In your small saucepan on low temp, warm the honey and almond butter till smooth. Remove, then mix in the vanilla extract.

4. Pour it into your oat mixture bowl, then mix well. Press it firmly into your lined baking pan. Bake for twenty mins till edges are golden brown. Cool it down, then slice into bars.

Tips: To make it nut-free, substitute almond butter with sunflower seed butter.

Serving size: One bar

Nutritional values (per serving): Calories: 180; Fat: 9g; Carbs: 22g; Protein: 4g; Sodium: 25mg; Sugar: 12g; Cholesterol: 0mg; Fiber: 3g

53. Oven-Baked Zucchini Fries

Preparation time: Ten mins

Cooking time: Twenty mins

Servings: Four

Ingredients:

- Two medium zucchinis cut into fries
- Half cup breadcrumbs
- Quarter cup Parmesan cheese, grated
- One tsp powdered garlic
- One tsp Italian seasoning
- One egg beaten
- One tbsp olive oil

Directions:

1. Warm up your oven to 425°F (220°C).
2. In your container, mix breadcrumbs, Parmesan, powdered garlic, and Italian seasoning. Dip zucchini fries first in the beaten egg and then coat with the breadcrumb mixture.
3. Place zucchini fries on your lined and greased baking sheet. Bake for twenty mins till golden brown, flipping halfway through.

Tips: For extra crispiness, broil for an additional two mins on high at the end of baking.

Serving size: One cup zucchini fries

Nutritional values (per serving): Calories: 100; Fat: 6g; Carbs: 10g; Protein: 5g; Sodium: 180mg; Sugar: 2g; Cholesterol: 40mg; Fiber: 2g

54.Homemade Trail Mix with Nuts and Seeds

Preparation time: Five mins

Cooking time: N/A

Servings: 6

Ingredients:

- One cup almonds
- One cup cashews
- Half cup pumpkin seeds
- Half cup sunflower seeds
- Half cup dried cranberries
- Half cup dark chocolate chips (optional)

Directions:

1. In your big container, mix almonds, cashews, pumpkin seeds, sunflower seeds, dried cranberries, and dark chocolate chips.
2. Mix well till everything is evenly distributed. Divide into individual servings.

Tips: For added variety, include other dried fruits such as apricots or raisins. Choose unsalted nuts and seeds to keep the sodium content low.

Serving size: Quarter cup

Nutritional values (per serving): Calories: 220; Fat: 14g; Carbs: 18g; Protein: 7g; Sodium: 10mg; Sugar: 9g; Cholesterol: 0mg

55.Stuffed Celery Sticks with Almond Butter

Preparation time: Ten mins

Cooking time: N/A

Servings: Four

Ingredients:

- Two cups celery sticks (about eight large sticks)
- One-half cup almond butter
- Two tbsp raisins
- Two tbsp sunflower seeds

Directions:

1. Wash and cut celery sticks into approximately three-inch pieces.
2. Spread about one tbsp almond butter into the hollow part of each celery stick.
3. Sprinkle raisins and sunflower seeds over the almond butter.

Tips: For added variety, try topping with chopped nuts or dried cranberries.

Serving size: Two stuffed celery sticks

Nutritional values (per serving): Calories: 150; Fat: 11g; Carbs: 12g; Protein: 4g; Sodium: 70mg; Sugar: 6g; Cholesterol: 0mg; Fiber: 3g

56. Baked Sweet Potato Chips

Preparation time: Ten mins

Cooking time: Twenty mins

Servings: Four

Ingredients:

- Two medium sweet potatoes
- One tbsp olive oil
- One tsp sea salt
- One-half tsp paprika

Directions:

1. Warm up your oven to 400°F (200°C).
2. Wash and thinly slice the sweet potatoes using a mandoline or sharp knife.
3. In your container, mix sweet potato slices and oil. Spread them on your lined baking sheet.
4. Sprinkle sea salt and paprika over the slices. Bake for fifteen to twenty mins or till crispy, turning halfway through.

Tips: For even baking, ensure all slices are similarly thick.

Serving size: Half a cup chips

Nutritional values (per serving): Calories: 120; Fat: 4g; Carbs: 20g; Protein: 1g; Sodium: 160mg; Sugar: 4g; Cholesterol: 0mg; Fiber: 3g

57. Edamame with Sea Salt

Preparation time: Five mins

Cooking time: Ten mins

Servings: Four

Ingredients:

- Two cups edamame (soybeans in pods)
- One tsp sea salt

Directions:

1. Let pot of water boil. Add the edamame and boil for five mins. Drain the edamame and place in your container.
2. Sprinkle sea salt over the edamame and toss well. Serve.

Tips: Serve warm for best flavor. You can add a pinch of chili flakes for an extra kick.

Serving size: One cup

Nutritional values (per serving): Calories: 120; Fat: 5g; Carbs: 10g; Protein: 8g; Sodium: 230mg; Sugar: 2g; Cholesterol: 0mg; Fiber: 4g

58. Quinoa and Kale Mini Muffins

Preparation time: Ten mins

Cooking time: Twenty mins

Servings: Twelve mini muffins

Ingredients:

- One cup cooked quinoa
- One cup chopped kale
- Two eggs, beaten
- Half cup grated Parmesan cheese
- One tbsp olive oil
- Half tsp powdered garlic
- Half tsp baking powder

Directions:

1. Warm up your oven to 350°F (175°C).
2. In your big container, combine quinoa, kale, eggs, Parmesan cheese, olive oil, powdered garlic, and baking powder.
3. Spoon it into your greased mini muffin tin. Bake for about twenty mins or till golden brown on top. Cool it down before removing from tin.

Tips: Ensure quinoa is completely cool before mixing with other ingredients. You can add some chopped onions for an additional flavor boost.

Serving size: One mini muffin

Nutritional values (per serving): Calories: 70; Fat: 3g; Carbs: 7g; Protein: 3g; Sodium: 100mg; Sugar: 1g; Cholesterol: 25mg; Fiber: 1g

CHAPTER 8

Guilt-free Sweet Treats

59. Spiced Pear Compote

Preparation time: Ten mins

Cooking time: Fifteen mins

Servings: Four

Ingredients:

- Four ripe pears, peeled, cored, and chopped
- One cup water
- Two tbsp lemon juice
- Two tbsp honey
- One tsp ground cinnamon
- Half tsp ground ginger
- Quarter tsp ground cloves

Directions:

1. In your medium saucepan, mix water, lemon juice, honey, cinnamon, ginger, and cloves. Add pears, then mix well. Let it boil on moderate-high temp.
2. Adjust to low temp, then simmer for fifteen mins till pears are tender. Remove, then cool slightly before serving.

Tips: Enjoy this compote warm or cold; it pairs excellently with yogurt or oatmeal.

Serving size: Half-cup

Nutritional values (per serving): Calories: 100; Fat: 0g; Carbs: 26g; Protein: 0g; Sodium: 5mg; Sugar: 20g; Cholesterol: 0mg; Fiber: 4g

60. Sweet Potato Brownies

Preparation time: Fifteen mins

Cooking time: Thirty mins

Servings: Eight

Ingredients:

- One cup mashed sweet potatoes
- One-half cup almond butter
- One-quarter cup unsweetened cocoa powder
- One-quarter cup maple syrup
- One tsp vanilla extract
- One tsp baking powder
- One-quarter tsp salt

Directions:

1. Warm up your oven to 350°F (175°C).
2. In your big container, mix mashed sweet potatoes, almond butter, maple syrup, and vanilla till smooth.
3. Add the cocoa powder, baking powder, and salt, then mix well. Pour it into your lined baking pan, then spread it out evenly.
4. Bake for thirty mins, then cool it down before slicing.

Tips: For extra sweetness, add one-quarter cup chocolate chips to the batter before baking.

Serving size: One brownie

Nutritional values (per serving): Calories: 130; Fat: 7g; Carbs: 16g; Protein: 3g; Sodium: 50mg; Sugar: 8g; Cholesterol: 0mg; Fiber: 3g

61. Frozen Yogurt Bark with Mixed Berries

Preparation time: Ten mins + freezing time

Cooking time: N/A

Servings: Eight

Ingredients:

- Two cups Greek yogurt (plain or flavored)
- Two tbsp honey or maple syrup
- Half cup mixed berries (strawberries, blueberries, raspberries)
- One-quarter cup granola
- One tsp vanilla extract

Directions:

1. In your medium container, mix yogurt, honey, and vanilla till blended. Spread it onto your lined baking sheet to about half an inch thickness.
2. Sprinkle mixed berries and granola evenly over the yogurt layer. Put baking sheet in your freezer for at least two hours or till completely frozen.
3. Break into pieces and serve immediately.

Tips: Feel free to use any mix of berries you prefer.

Serving size: One piece

Nutritional values (per serving): Calories: 90; Fat: 2g; Carbs: 12g; Protein: 5g; Sodium: 40mg; Sugar: 7g; Cholesterol: 5mg; Fiber: 1g

62. Lemon Chia Seed Cookies

Preparation time: Fifteen mins

Cooking time: Ten mins

Servings: Twelve cookies

Ingredients:

- One cup almond flour
- Quarter cup coconut flour
- Two tbsp chia seeds
- Quarter cup honey
- Juiced and zested from one lemon
- One egg
- Quarter cup coconut oil, melted

Directions:

1. Warm up your oven to 350°F (175°C).

2. In your container, mix all flours, and chia seeds. Add the honey, lemon juice, zest, egg, and oil, then mix well.
3. Scoop tablespoon-sized amounts of dough onto your lined baking sheet. Flatten each cookie slightly using your fork.
4. Bake for ten mins till the edges are golden brown. Cool it down, then serve.

Tips: Add a touch of vanilla extract for extra flavor.

Serving size: 1 cookie

Nutritional values (per serving): Calories: 90; Fat: 7g; Carbs: 7g; Protein: 2g; Sodium: 15mg; Sugar: 6g; Cholesterol: 10mg; Fiber: 2g

63. Peanut Butter and Banana Nice Cream

Preparation time: Ten mins + freezing time

Cooking time: N/A

Servings: Four

Ingredients:

- Three ripe bananas, sliced and frozen
- Quarter cup natural peanut butter
- One tbsp honey (optional)
- Quarter cup unsweetened almond milk

Directions:

1. Put frozen banana slices in your food processor or blender. Blend on high till bananas become crumbly.
2. Add the peanut butter, honey (if using), and almond milk. Continue blending till smooth. Freeze for one to two hours for firmer texture.

Tips: Garnish with chopped nuts or cacao nibs for added crunch. For a chocolate twist, add one tbsp cocoa powder before blending.

Serving size: Half cup

Nutritional values (per serving): Calories: 150; Fat: 7g; Carbs: 21g; Protein: 4g; Sodium: 40mg; Sugar: 13g; Cholesterol: 0mg; Fiber: 3g

64.Avocado and Lime Cheesecake

Preparation time: Twenty mins + chilling time

Cooking time: N/A

Servings: Eight

Ingredients:

- Two ripe avocados, mashed
- One cup cream cheese, softened
- Half cup honey
- Quarter cup lime juice
- One tbsp lime zest
- One tsp vanilla extract
- One premade graham cracker crust

Directions:

1. In your mixing container, blend the mashed avocados and cream cheese till smooth. Add honey, lime juice, lime zest, and vanilla extract. Mix well.
2. Pour the avocado-lime mixture into the premade graham cracker crust. Smooth the top with a spatula, then refrigerate for at least two hours. Serve.

Tips: For added texture, sprinkle a bit of lime zest on top before refrigerating. Use ripe avocados for the best flavor.

Serving size: 1 slice

Nutritional values (per serving): Calories: 250; Fat: 18g; Carbs: 20g; Protein: 4g; Sodium: 150mg; Sugar: 15g; Cholesterol: 30mg; Fiber: 3g

65.Almond Flour Chocolate Chip Cookies

Preparation time: Ten mins

Cooking time: Twelve mins

Servings: Twelve

Ingredients:

- Two cups almond flour
- Quarter cup coconut oil or butter, melted
- Quarter cup honey or maple syrup
- Half tsp baking soda
- One tsp vanilla extract
- Pinch of salt
- Half cup dark chocolate chips

Directions:

1. Warm up your oven to 350°F (175°C).
2. In your container, mix flour, oil, honey, baking soda, vanilla extract, and salt. Fold in the dark chocolate chips.
3. Scoop tablespoon-sized amounts of dough onto your lined baking sheet and flatten slightly with your hands.
4. Bake for twelve mins or till the edges are lightly golden brown. Cool it down, then serve.

Tips: Use high-quality dark chocolate chips for richer flavor.

Serving size: 1 cookie

Nutritional values (per serving): Calories: 150; Fat: 12g; Carbs: 10g; Protein: 3g; Sodium: 60mg; Sugar: 6g; Cholesterol: varies based on oil/butter used; Fiber: 2g

66. *Strawberry and Oat Crumble*

Preparation time: Ten mins

Cooking time: Thirty mins

Servings: Four

Ingredients:

- One cup rolled oats
- Half cup almond flour
- Quarter cup maple syrup
- Quarter cup coconut oil (melted)
- One pound strawberries (hulled and sliced)
- Two tbsp chia seeds
- One tsp lemon juice

Directions:

1. Warm up your oven to 350°F (175°C).
2. In your mixing container, mix oats, flour, maple syrup, and oil. Mix till crumbly.
3. In another bowl, toss the sliced strawberries with chia seeds and lemon juice.
4. Spread the strawberry mixture evenly in your baking dish, then sprinkle the oat crumble on top.   Bake for thirty mins or till golden brown.

Tips: Serve warm with some Greek yogurt or a scoop of vanilla ice cream for extra indulgence.

Serving size: One-fourth of the crumble

Nutritional values (per serving): Calories: 200; Fat: 10g; Carbs: 30g; Protein: 3g; Sodium: 5mg; Sugar: 14g; Cholesterol: 0mg; Fiber: 5g

67. Carrot Cake Energy Balls

Preparation time: Fifteen mins + chilling time

Cooking time: N/A

Servings: Six

Ingredients:

- One cup carrots, shredded
- Half cup rolled oats
- Third cup almond butter
- Quarter cup raisins
- Quarter cup unsweetened shredded coconut
- Two tbsp honey or maple syrup
- Half tsp cinnamon

Directions:

1. In a food processor, mix carrots, oats, almond butter, raisins, shredded coconut, honey or maple syrup, and cinnamon.
2. Pulse till well combined and the mixture is sticky. Roll into one-inch balls, then put them on your lined baking sheet.
3. Chill in the refrigerator for at least one hour.

Tips: Store in an airtight container in the fridge for up to one week.

Serving size: Two balls

Nutritional values (per serving): Calories: 150; Fat: 7g; Carbs: 19g; Protein: 4g; Sodium: 40mg; Sugar: 8g; Cholesterol: 0mg; Fiber: 3g

68. *Cashew and Date Energy Bars*

Preparation time: Fifteen mins

Cooking time: N/A

Servings: Twelve bars

Ingredients:

- Two cups pitted dates
- One cup raw cashews
- Half cup rolled oats
- Two tbsp chia seeds
- One tsp vanilla extract
- A pinch of salt

Directions:

1. In your food processor, blend pitted dates till a sticky ball forms. Add the raw cashews, rolled oats, chia seeds, vanilla extract, and salt. Blend till well combined.
2. Press the mixture evenly into the lined pan. Refrigerate for at least an hour before slicing into bars.

Tips: For extra flavor, you can toast the cashews and oats before blending.

Serving size: 1 bar

Nutritional values (per serving): Calories: 180; Fat: 9g; Carbs: 23g; Protein: 3g; Sodium: 30mg; Sugar: 15g; Cholesterol: 0mg; Fiber: 4g

69. *Raw Caramel Slice*

Preparation time: Twenty mins + chilling time

Cooking time: N/A

Servings: Ten slices

Ingredients:

- Two cups medjool dates, pitted

- One cup raw almonds
- Half cup coconut oil, melted
- One third cup pure maple syrup
- One tsp vanilla extract
- A pinch of sea salt

Directions:

1. For the base layer, blend one cup pitted dates with raw almonds till combined but still slightly chunky. Press this mixture firmly into your lined loaf pan.
2. For the caramel layer, blend the remaining one cup dates with melted coconut oil, pure maple syrup, vanilla, and sea salt till smooth.
3. Spread the caramel layer evenly over the base layer. Refrigerate for at least two hours or till firm before slicing.

Tips: Keep refrigerated to maintain texture and freshness. Use a sharp knife for clean slices.

Serving size: 1 slice

Nutritional values (per serving): Calories: 210; Fat: 14g; Carbs: 22g; Protein: 3g; Sodium: 45mg; Sugar: 16g; Cholesterol: 0mg; Fiber: 3g

70. *Orange and Almond Flour Cake*

Preparation time: Ten mins

Cooking time: Forty mins

Servings: Eight

Ingredients:

- Two cups almond flour
- Three eggs
- Half cup honey
- Zest of two oranges
- Quarter cup fresh orange juice (juice from one orange)
- One tsp baking powder
- One tsp vanilla extract

Directions:

1. Warm up your oven to 350°F (175°C).

2. In your big container, whisk eggs, honey, zest, orange juice, and vanilla. Add almond flour and baking powder, then mix till smooth.

3. Pour the batter into your lined cake pan. Bake for forty mins, cool it down, then serve.

Tips: Garnish with orange slices or a light dusting of powdered sugar before serving.

Serving size: One slice

Nutritional values (per serving): Calories: 250; Fat: 18g; Carbs: 18g; Protein: 8g; Sodium: 60mg; Sugar: 14g; Cholesterol: 60mg ; Fiber: 3g

CHAPTER 9

Refreshing Beverages for Any Time

71. Chocolate and Peanut Butter Protein Shake

Preparation time: Five mins

Cooking time: N/A

Servings: Two

Ingredients:

- Two cups unsweetened almond milk
- One tbsp unsweetened cocoa powder
- Two tbsp natural peanut butter
- One ripe banana
- Two scoops chocolate protein powder
- One tsp honey or maple syrup (optional)
- Six ice cubes

Directions:

1. Combine milk, cocoa powder, peanut butter, banana, protein powder, honey, and ice in your blender.
2. Blend till smooth. Pour into glasses and serve immediately.

Tips: For a thicker shake, add more ice cubes or a little frozen banana. Substitute almond milk with any other plant-based milk like soy or oat milk.

Serving size: One cup

Nutritional values (per serving): Calories: 250; Fat: 10g; Carbs: 20g; Protein: 25g; Sodium: 150mg; Sugar: 10g; Cholesterol: 0mg; Fiber: 4g

72. Cranberry and Apple Cider Vinegar Tonic

Preparation time: Three mins

Cooking time: N/A

Servings: Two

Ingredients:

- One cup unsweetened cranberry juice
- Two tbsp apple cider vinegar
- Two cups water
- One tbsp honey or maple syrup (optional)
- Ice cubes

Directions:

1. In a pitcher, mix cranberry juice, apple cider vinegar, and water. Stir well to mix.
2. Add honey or maple syrup if using, and stir till dissolved. Pour into glasses over ice cubes.

Tips: For extra flavor, add a splash of lemon juice or fresh mint leaves. Adjust sweetness to taste by varying the amount of honey or syrup.

Serving size: One cup

Nutritional values (per serving): Calories: 25; Fat: 0g; Carbs: 5g; Protein: 0g; Sodium: 10mg; Sugar: 5g; Cholesterol: 0mg; Fiber: 0g

73. Green Tea and Lemon Detox Drink

Preparation time: Five mins

Cooking time: N/A

Servings: Two

Ingredients:

- Two cups hot water
- Two green tea bags
- One tbsp lemon juice (freshly squeezed)
- One tsp honey (optional)
- Ice cubes

Directions:

1. Steep the green tea bags in the hot water for three to five mins. Remove the tea bags and let the tea cool down for a few mins.

2. Add freshly squeezed lemon juice to the tea. Stir in honey if desired. Pour the mixture into glasses filled with ice cubes.

Tips: Add a slice of lemon as a garnish for extra flavor. For a stronger detox effect, add a pinch of cayenne pepper.

Serving size: 1 cup

Nutritional values (per serving): Calories: 20; Fat: 0g; Carbs: 6g; Protein: 0g; Sodium: 0mg; Sugar: 5g; Cholesterol: 0mg; Fiber: 0g

74. *Cucumber and Mint Cooler*

Preparation time: Ten mins

Cooking time: N/A

Servings: Four

Ingredients:

- One sliced cucumber
- Quarter cup fresh mint leaves
- Juice of one lemon (about 3 tbsp)
- Four cups water
- Ice cubes

Directions:

1. In your pitcher, mix cucumber and fresh mint. Add lemon juice, pour in four cups water, then mix well.
2. Refrigerate for at least two hours to let the flavors meld together. Serve over ice cubes for a refreshingly cool drink.

Tips: For added flavor, you can add a few slices of lime or a splash of sparkling water before serving.

Serving size: 1 cup

Nutritional values (per serving): Calories: 10; Fat: 0g; Carbs: 2g; Protein: 0g; Sodium: 5mg; Sugar: <1g; Cholesterol: 0mg; Fiber: <1g

75. *Ginger and Lime Detox Water*

Preparation time: Five mins

Cooking time: N/A

Servings: Four

Ingredients:

- Two tsp grated ginger
- One lime, thinly sliced
- Eight cups water
- Four mint leaves (optional)

Directions:

1. In a large pitcher, mix water, grated ginger, and lime slices.
2. Stir well and let it sit for at least one hour in the refrigerator to allow flavors to infuse.
3. Add mint leaves before serving if desired.

Tips: For a stronger flavor, let the water infuse overnight in the refrigerator. You can use sparkling water for a fizzy twist.

Serving size: Two cups

Nutritional values (per serving): Calories: 5; Fat: 0g; Carbs: 1g; Protein: 0g; Sodium: 10mg; Sugar: 0g; Cholesterol: 0mg; Fiber: 0g

76. Avocado and Spinach Smoothie

Preparation time: Five mins

Cooking time: N/A

Servings: Two

Ingredients:

- One ripe avocado, scoop out the flesh
- One cup fresh spinach
- One cup unsweetened almond milk
- Two tbsp honey
- Half cup ice cubes
- One tbsp chia seeds

Directions:

1. In a blender, combine all ingredients till smooth.

2. Pour into glasses and enjoy immediately.

Tips: Add more almond milk if a thinner consistency is desired. For added protein, include one scoop of your preferred protein powder.

Serving size: One cup

Nutritional values (per serving): Calories: 230; Fat: 15g; Carbs: 23g; Protein: 3g; Sodium: 45mg; Sugar: 13g; Cholesterol: 0mg; Fiber: 8g

77. *Watermelon and Basil Cooler*

Preparation time: Ten mins

Cooking time: N/A

Servings: Four

Ingredients:

- Four cups watermelon, cubed
- Two tbsp fresh basil leaves, finely chopped
- One tbsp lemon juice
- One cup cold water
- Two tsp honey

Directions:

1. In a blender, mix watermelon cubes, basil leaves, lemon juice, cold water, and honey.
2. Blend till smooth. Pour into glasses and serve.

Tips: For an extra refreshing drink, chill the watermelon before blending. You can add ice cubes before blending for a slushier texture.

Serving size: One cup

Nutritional values (per serving): Calories: 50; Fat: 0g; Carbs: 13g; Protein: 1g; Sodium: 2mg; Sugar: 12g; Cholesterol: 0mg; Fiber: 1g

78. *Pomegranate and Green Tea Elixir*

Preparation time: Five mins

Cooking time: N/A

Servings: Four

Ingredients:

- Four cups brewed green tea, chilled
- Two cups pomegranate juice
- Two tsp honey
- One tbsp lemon juice

Directions:

1. Brew the green tea according to package instructions and chill in the refrigerator.
2. In a large pitcher, mix the chilled green tea with pomegranate juice, honey, and lemon juice.
3. Stir well to combine and dissolve the honey. Serve over ice if desired.

Tips: For added flavor, garnish with fresh mint leaves or pomegranate arils. Adjust the sweetness by adding more honey if necessary.

Serving size: One cup

Nutritional values (per serving): Calories: 45; Fat: 0g; Carbs: 12g; Protein: 0g; Sodium: 5mg; Sugar: 11g; Cholesterol: 0mg; Fiber: 0g

79. Lemon and Cayenne Pepper Detox Drink

Preparation time: Five mins

Cooking time: N/A

Servings: One

Ingredients:

- One cup water
- Two tbsp lemon juice (freshly squeezed)
- Half tsp cayenne pepper
- One tbsp maple syrup

Directions:

1. Pour the water into a glass. Add the lemon juice, cayenne pepper, and maple syrup.
2. Stir well till all ingredients are thoroughly mixed. Serve immediately.

Tips: For an extra boost, add a pinch of turmeric. Drink first thing in the morning on an empty stomach for best results.

Serving size: 1 cup

Nutritional values (per serving): Calories: 36; Fat: 0g; Carbs: 9g; Protein: 0g; Sodium: 5mg; Sugar: 8g; Cholesterol: 0mg; Fiber: 0g

80. Spirulina and Pineapple Smoothie

Preparation time: Five mins

Cooking time: N/A

Servings: One

Ingredients:

- One cup pineapple chunks
- One cup coconut water
- One tsp spirulina powder
- One tbsp chia seeds
- Half cup baby spinach leaves

Directions:

1. Add all ingredients to a blender. Blend till smooth.
2. Pour into a glass and serve immediately.

Tips: Use frozen pineapple for an extra chilled smoothie. Adjust coconut water quantity for desired consistency.

Serving size: 1 cup

Nutritional values (per serving): Calories: 140; Fat: 3g; Carbs: 30g; Protein: 3g; Sodium: 65mg; Sugar: 16g; Cholesterol: 0mg; Fiber: 6g

28-DAY MEAL PLAN

DAY	BREAKFAST	LUNCH	DINNER	SNACK/DESSERT
1	Berry Blast Smoothie Bowl	Quinoa and Avocado Power Bowl	Sweet Potato and Kale Stew	Spiced Pear Compote
2	Buckwheat Pancakes with Fresh Fruit	Greek Salad with Quinoa and Feta	Maple-Glazed Pork Chops with Sweet Potatoes	Roasted Almonds with Sea Salt
3	Tomato and Basil Breakfast Tartine	Roasted Red Pepper and Hummus Wrap	Mushroom and Tofu Stir-Fry	Orange and Almond Flour Cake
4	Matcha Green Tea Smoothie Bowl	Asian-Inspired Salmon Poke Bowl	Vegan Cauliflower Tacos	Stuffed Celery Sticks with Almond Butter
5	Cottage Cheese with Fresh Berries and Honey	Turkey and Avocado Club Wrap	Healthy Turkey Meatloaf	Raw Caramel Slice
6	Mixed Nut and Seed Breakfast Bars	Hearty Minestrone Soup	Baked Cod with Tomato Basil Sauce	Quinoa and Kale Mini Muffins
7	Savory Oatmeal with Avocado and Poached Egg	Tuna and Spinach Whole Wheat Sandwich	Turkey and Spinach Stuffed Shells	Cashew and Date Energy Bars
8	Tofu Scramble with Peppers and Onions	Sweet Potato and Black Bean Buddha Bowl	Cauliflower Mac and Cheese	Edamame with Sea Salt
9	Spinach and Mushroom Frittata	Vegetable and Quinoa Stew	Rosemary Roasted Chicken with Root Vegetables	Strawberry and Oat Crumble
10	Apple and Cinnamon Quinoa Bowl	Hummus and Veggie Whole Grain Wrap	Moroccan-Spiced Vegetable Tagine	Baked Sweet Potato Chips
11	Egg White and Veggie Omelette	Grilled Chicken and Mango Salad	Spicy Chicken and Veggie Skewers	Carrot Cake Energy Balls

12	Pumpkin Spice Breakfast Muffins	Butternut Squash and Lentil Soup	Black Bean and Sweet Potato Enchiladas	Mini Caprese Skewers
13	Almond Butter and Banana Toast	Grilled Chicken and Pesto Panini	Teriyaki Chicken with Steamed Veggies	Sweet Potato Brownies
14	Coconut and Blueberry Overnight Oats	Chicken and Wild Rice Soup	Vegan Thai Green Curry with Tofu	Homemade Trail Mix with Nuts and Seeds
15	Protein-Packed Breakfast Burrito	Mediterranean Lentil Salad	Baked Zucchini Lasagna	Almond Flour Chocolate Chip Cookies
16	Berry Blast Smoothie Bowl	Quinoa and Avocado Power Bowl	Sweet Potato and Kale Stew	Oven-Baked Zucchini Fries
17	Buckwheat Pancakes with Fresh Fruit	Greek Salad with Quinoa and Feta	Maple-Glazed Pork Chops with Sweet Potatoes	Avocado and Lime Cheesecake
18	Tomato and Basil Breakfast Tartine	Roasted Red Pepper and Hummus Wrap	Mushroom and Tofu Stir-Fry	Pumpkin Seed and Cranberry Bars
19	Matcha Green Tea Smoothie Bowl	Asian-Inspired Salmon Poke Bowl	Vegan Cauliflower Tacos	Frozen Yogurt Bark with Mixed Berries
20	Cottage Cheese with Fresh Berries and Honey	Turkey and Avocado Club Wrap	Healthy Turkey Meatloaf	Carrot and Apple Slaw
21	Mixed Nut and Seed Breakfast Bars	Hearty Minestrone Soup	Baked Cod with Tomato Basil Sauce	Peanut Butter and Banana Nice Cream
22	Savory Oatmeal with Avocado and Poached Egg	Tuna and Spinach Whole Wheat Sandwich	Turkey and Spinach Stuffed Shells	Blueberry and Oat Energy Bars
23	Tofu Scramble with Peppers and Onions	Sweet Potato and Black Bean Buddha Bowl	Cauliflower Mac and Cheese	Lemon Chia Seed Cookies
24	Spinach and Mushroom	Vegetable and	Rosemary Roasted Chicken with Root	Spiced Pumpkin

	Frittata	Quinoa Stew	Vegetables	Seeds
25	Apple and Cinnamon Quinoa Bowl	Hummus and Veggie Whole Grain Wrap	Moroccan-Spiced Vegetable Tagine	Cucumber and Hummus Roll-Ups
26	Egg White and Veggie Omelette	Grilled Chicken and Mango Salad	Spicy Chicken and Veggie Skewers	Spiced Pear Compote
27	Pumpkin Spice Breakfast Muffins	Butternut Squash and Lentil Soup	Black Bean and Sweet Potato Enchiladas	Roasted Almonds with Sea Salt
28	Almond Butter and Banana Toast	Grilled Chicken and Pesto Panini	Teriyaki Chicken with Steamed Veggies	Orange and Almond Flour Cake

CONCLUSION

The Good Energy Cookbook has been an exciting journey into understanding how better food choices can transform your life. We've learned a lot about what is metabolism and its powerful role in energy levels. We've busted myths, embraced the benefits of a good energy diet, and dived deep into the impact of nutrition on our metabolic health. These foundations aren't just scientific facts—they're practical tools you can use daily. By focusing on nutrient-dense foods and balanced meals that stabilize blood sugar levels, you can keep your energy steady throughout the day.

Stocking your kitchen with good energy foods was another crucial milestone. From superfoods that revitalize you to pantry staples that make healthy eating more accessible, creating a well-stocked kitchen sets the stage for dietary success. We've seen how having these ingredients at hand encourages you to make better food choices without feeling deprived or overwhelmed.

The recipes were crafted to support every part of your day, from morning boosts like flavorful smoothies and hearty breakfast options to power-packed lunches and wholesome dinners. Whether it's a *Berry Blast Smoothie Bowl* to kickstart your morning or a *Sweet Potato and Black Bean Buddha Bowl* for lunch, each recipe is designed to maximize energy and sustain you throughout your tasks.

Snacks also play a vital role when it comes to maintaining energy levels between meals. Knowing what to grab when hunger strikes can make all the difference. Energy-boosting snacks like *Roasted Almonds with Sea Salt* or *Blueberry and Oat Energy Bars* keep you satisfied without the sugar crash that comes with unhealthy snacking.

The focus on guilt-free treats ensures that indulging doesn't have to derail your health goals. Delights like *Avocado and Lime Cheesecake* or *Peanut Butter and Banana Nice Cream* show that you can enjoy sweet moments while still giving your body what it needs to thrive. Finally, refreshing beverages add another layer of nourishment. From detoxifying *Green Tea* and *Lemon* drinks to revitalizing Avocado and Spinach Smoothies, these drinks not only quench thirst but also provide essential nutrients to keep you going strong.

Your journey doesn't end here. The principles you've learned from this cookbook are stepping stones. Keep experimenting with new recipes, listening to your body's signals, and enjoying the process of feeding yourself well.

Good energy is more than just a diet—it's a lifestyle of choices that honor both your taste buds and your wellbeing. So, embrace each small step forward, celebrate your progress, and carry these lessons with you for life-long vitality. Don't forget to enjoy the process!

MEASUREMENTS & CONVERSIONS

VOLUME EQUIVALENTS (LIQUID)		
US STANDARD	**US OUNCES**	**METRIC (APPROX.)**
1 teaspoon	1/6 oz	5 ml
1 tablespoon	1/2 oz	15 ml
1 fluid ounce	1 oz	30 ml
1 cup	8 oz	240 ml
1 pint	16 oz	475 ml
1 quart	32 oz	950 ml
1 gallon	128 oz	3.8 L

VOLUME EQUIVALENTS (DRY)		WEIGHT EQUIVALENTS	
US STANDARD	**METRIC (APPROX.)**	**US STANDARD**	**METRIC (APPROX.)**
1/4 teaspoon	1.25 ml	1 ounce	28 g
1/2 teaspoon	2.5 ml	4 ounces	113 g
1 teaspoon	5 ml	8 ounces	225 g
1/4 cup	60 ml	12 ounces	340 g
1/3 cup	80 ml	One pound (16oz)	455 g
1/2 cup	120 ml		
1 cup	240 ml		

OVEN TEMPERATURES	
FAHRENHEIT	**CELSIUS (APPROX.)**
200° F	93° C
225° F	107° C
250° F	121° C
275° F	135° C
300° F	149° C
325° F	163° C
350° F	177° C
375°F	191° C
400°F	204° C
425°F	218°C

Note: The values in the tables are approximate and should be used for reference as a guide when cooking.

Made in the USA
Thornton, CO
12/31/24 06:27:36

3a41a6c7-91cb-4974-92ff-333bcba71db3R01